The Ups and Downs of being in your 40s

The Ups and Downs of being in your 40s

Tony Husband

AURA

This edition published in 2017
by Baker & Taylor UK Ltd,
Bicester, Oxfordshire, OX26 4ST

Copyright © Arcturus Holdings Limited/Tony Husband
26/27 Bickels Yard, 151–153 Bermondsey Street
London SE1 3HA

ISBN: 978-1-78828-802-6
AD006042UK

Printed in China

INTRODUCTION

Bob Hope said you know you're getting old when the candles cost more than your birthday cake. But being in your 40s isn't old, is it? Of course, you may have to make a few adjustments, like perfecting your comb-over, getting yourself some nice, elasticized slacks and learning to sleep in your socks. Accept it, you're slowly turning into your parents. You're built for comfort not speed now.

In truth, my 40s were golden years. I was employed as a full-time cartoonist, my work was in demand and I was prolific enough to be able to afford a nice house with a big garden ideal for a young family. Trips to London became frequent and life opened up. I joined the Groucho Club in its heyday with all the madness that came with it. My social life expanded to a crazy level as I got to know more and more people. I was living in the land of rock'n'roll, which was perhaps what led *The Times* to call me the Keith Richards of cartooning. I burned the candle at both ends – as well as in the middle – and got away with it. You could back then!

It's harder to be 40 now. There are so many new things to worry about. How do you keep up with the people whose lives seem beyond perfect on Facebook? How can you be cool when you still live with your parents? At what age should you stop wearing jeans? You won't find the answers in this book, but if you recognize the situations and smile, that's good enough for me.

Tony Husband

'It's official, darling: the 40s are the new 30s.'

'Fancy going for a drink?'

'Yes, but does your personal trainer have to be half your age?'

'I'll choose the au pair thank you very much!'

'I've reached the age where I'm ripe for counselling.'

'John, wake up... I'm 43; you're 45:
I've decided we'll become vegans!'

'The thing is I don't feel nearly as old as I thought I would.'

'Now we're in our 40s, isn't it time to look for a static caravan?'

'I found some hair in the shower. It can't be mine.
Please tell me you've been showering the dog again.'

'Have you noticed how, now they've hit their 40s,
we get a lot fewer walks?'

'Do you have anything to invigorate a man of a certain age?'

'I doubt very much your trousers have shrunk, Matt.'

'I don't care whether it's Merlot, Malbec or Mataro
as long as it's strong.'

'Yawning when it's time to buy your round? Ha! You never did that in your 30s.'

'Hi, mate. No, I can't afford to come out for a drink.
It's the "Ex-Factor". I'm broke!'

'Just started my bucket list: by the time I'm 41 I'll have bungee-jumped in New Zealand; by 42 — gone over the Niagara Falls in a barrel; by 43 — swum with dolphins; by 44 —'

'Not so much crow's feet as canary tiptoes. Looking good, girl!'

'Bad news! We can't go on Under-40s holidays any more.'

'I'm joining a gym to tone up.' 'Tell me: are you having an affair?'

'Being too old to rock and roll isn't the end of the world, Roger.'

'14 units of alcohol a week?! I was sure it was per day.'

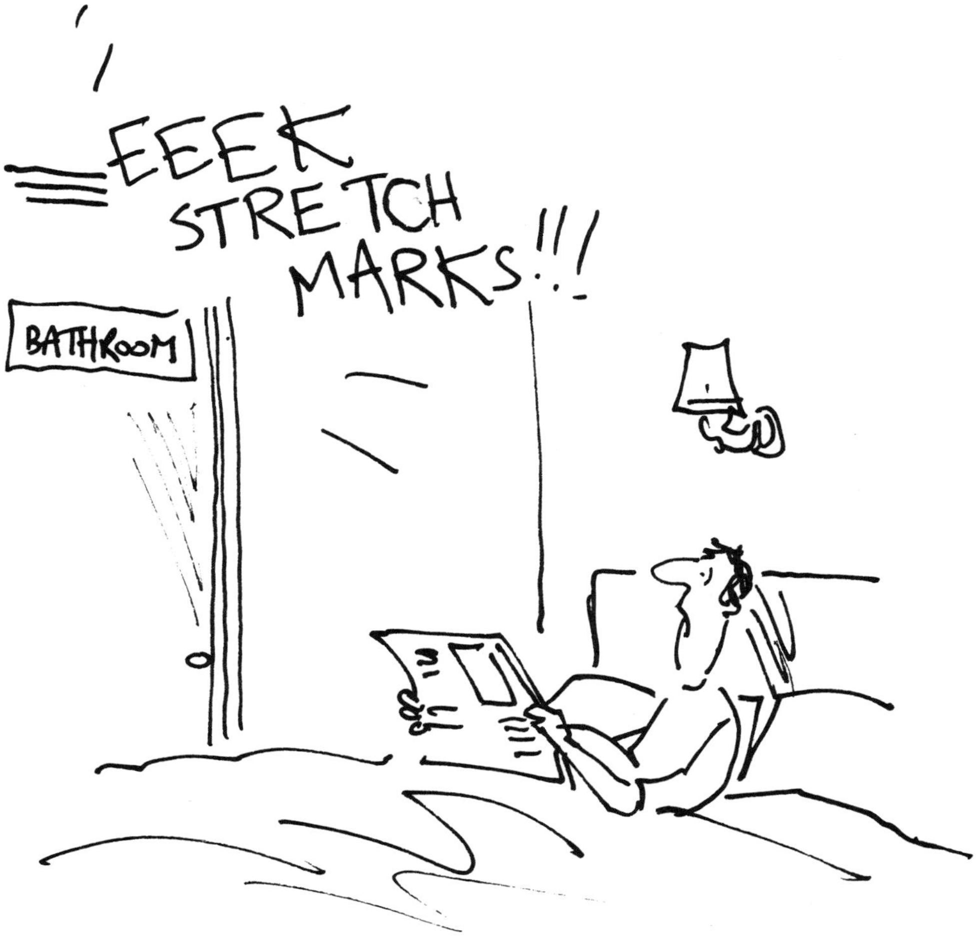
EEEK STRETCH MARKS!!!
BATHROOM

'Son, now you're 45, your mother and I were wondering if you'd ever thought of finding a place of your own?'

'Don't ask me my age. I never use the "F" word.'

'Did you never fancy having children?'

'We've still got another half to go!'

'It's from the wife upstairs in bed: can we keep the noise down?!'

'So long, lads. Thanks for the good times.'

'You're in your 40s?! Wow, cool!'

'Darling, wake up... I've decided I'm going to climb Everest.'

'I'm trying to keep my waist size below my age.'

'We don't talk any more, just text.'

'So we're vegetarian now, are we? Er, since when?'

'You've got absolutely no idea just how serious man flu is.'

'You can't come home, son. Your dad's turned your bedroom into a gym.'

'Scuse me, at what age should a man stop wearing jeans?'

'Sadly, burning the candle at both ends is no longer an option at your age.'

'I've made an executive decision, Ralph:
we ditch the sports car and get a people carrier.'

'I bet my dad's got more tattoos than your dad.'

'Hey, Joe, remember when we played football on Saturday mornings.'

'Is this our future now?'

'I can't remember: is it cooler for guys to date older women or the other way round?'

'I don't know, perhaps we should be thinking about
a more practical car now.'

'Blimey, when she's 10, you'll be 55... that's ancient.'

'Now we're over 40, could you let me drive occasionally?'

'Scuse me, I'm looking for an older woman with experience.'

'Stop saying, "Word on the street" and "My bad". You're a 46-year-old man who lives in a cul-de-sac, whose hobby is gardening and who drinks cocoa before bed-time.'

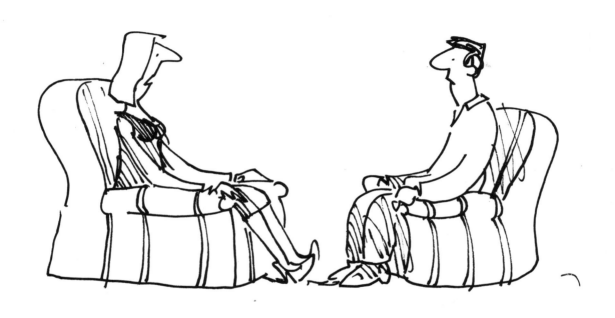

'I think you look more in your 40s than I do.'

'You're thinking of filling my position with someone younger?!
But I'm only 45!!'

'Oh no! Did I really just say today's pop music is rubbish?!'

'Aagh, my parents have bought me a cardigan.'

'Hope you don't mind me saying so, darling, but you're not the surfer dude you once were.'

'I thought by my mid-40s I'd have a home, freedom, space, but no,
I'm stuck at my parents' house.'

'Seems our rave days are over. That was Tamsin and Tom
inviting us to a Scrabble night.'

'Groan... it's not the late nights I'm finding difficult;
it's the mornings after.'

'George, quick. Suddenly, I find I'm in my 40s!!
At least tell me I don't look it!'

'Aaaagh! I've just had a nightmare about our mortgage!'

'Ha... I never knew you were hiding a bald patch.'

'I'm in my 40s now. The clock's well and truly ticking.'

'He says he wants stories with more gratuitous violence
like the babysitter tells him.'

'Right, turn off that rubbish you're watching. I've bought a boxset of keep-fit videos for the over-40s.'

'I used to think people in their 40s were ancient.'

'They say life begins at 40, Puss. Hasn't happened to me yet.'

'OK, OK, I know I'm showing my age, but next door's putting rubbish in the wrong bin again.'

'I forget, Tessa. Is it my laser eye treatment or my teeth whitening appointment today?'

'I think I'm having a midlife crisis. I can't stop going to Glastonbury.'

'I know she's sound asleep, but can you check if there's a monster
under the bed for me?'

'For my 45th birthday, I'm thinking of buying a new set of golf clubs:
Wentworth, the Belfry, Sunningdale...'

'Do you have anything on your books with a three-mile gravel drive, croquet lawn and an orangery?'

'Yes, admittedly we're 40 somethings, but very rich 40 somethings!'

'Madame, just think how well this gorgeous Gucci bag would go with your elegance, your age and your bank account.'

'I agree with getting a dog, Nick, but not just any old dog!
Something with a bit of class...'

'Look, Dad, there's your other house.'

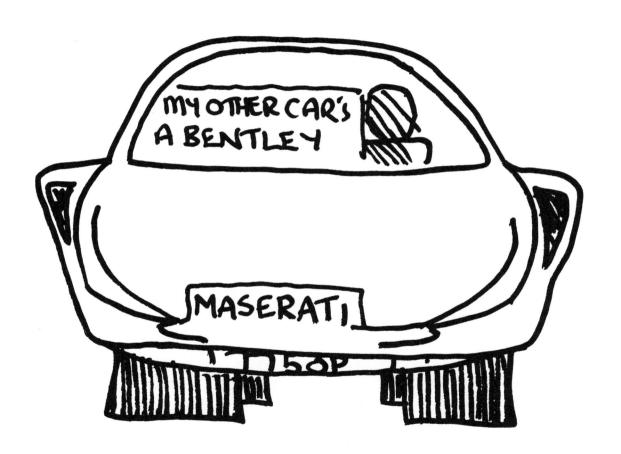

'It's Tim and Julie. They're having a party tonight. If we can't get a babysitter, can I go on my own please?'

'Tequila slammers at our age! Are you sure?'

'All my friends have got kids. But I've got you, Bruno.'

'Fancy forming a middle-aged boy band?'

'Can't remember: is it trendy or not trendy to have a beard?'

'Mummy, mummy, mummy, Jenny at school's mum is in her 40s.
You aren't, are you?'

'She prefers older men... some of them as old as 40.'

'Let's go, Tom. No one here is the right age for us.'

'Hold on there just a minute: I'm only in my 40s. Why would I need life insurance?'

'I've had my first afternoon nap.'

'Of course, we're very proud of your wonderful career, darling, but a tiny part of us is sad we're not blessed with grandchildren.'

'Sorry we're late. He was trying to get into some of his, erm, older trousers.'

'Gasp, I think it's time to take up Crown Green bowling.'

'That was Molly; she's just left me.'

'So he says, "I'm gonna get a tattoo of the love of my life."
I was thinking that's really sweet of him, but now he's gone and got
"UNITED" printed across his back.'

'Your jeans are too tight; your face has gone blue.'

'You should get your wife to shave your back like I do, mate.'

'Aaagh! Nose hairs!'

'Great news, I'm resurrecting my old vinyl collection!'

'For goodness sake, will someone please ask her how
the teeth whitening went?'

'I'm not sure I've successfully made the leap
from my 30s to my 40s.'

'OK, listen. Our Joe's split up with Debbie. She's keeping the flat and he's moving back in with us. Isn't that great?'

'Dear Mum and Dad, don't worry about me. I've got a couple of lovely friends.'

'I've reached an age where I could have a toy boy.'

'Son, are you going to be OK in a flat on your own? You're only 41.'

'Turn that music down. Aaagh! Sorry, son, forget it.
I'm sounding like my dad.'

'Oh no, I just looked in the bathroom mirror and saw my dad staring back at me.'

'Funny how we're drawn more to the wines these days.'

'Sorry we're late. We were just watching Peppa Pig with the kids.'

'The older I get, the more I look like the dog.'

'This is my school diary: "Prediction -- by my 45th birthday I will have walked on the Moon."'

'As I get older, I seem to spend more and more time at your surgery. My wife thinks we're having an affair.'

'I imagine being a single mum in your 40s is much harder.'

'Psst... anti-wrinkle cream, please.'

'43 and just been asked for ID... Get in there!'

'No way, you're never in your 40s.'

'Dad, you're in your 40s now. Don't you think you should be cutting down on the wine?'

'I'm not giving in to this age thing. Gasp!'

'We had a choice, children or dogs. We chose the latter.'

'What do you mean, no over-35s?'

'Do you remember when we used to go out to enjoy ourselves?'

Gently Where the Roads Go

BY ALAN HUNTER

CASSELL · LONDON

CASSELL & COMPANY LTD

35 Red Lion Square · London WC1

and at

MELBOURNE · SYDNEY · TORONTO
JOHANNESBURG · CAPE TOWN · AUCKLAND

———

Printed in Great Britain by
The Camelot Press Ltd., London and Southampton
F.362

For my Son or Daughter,
as the event proves

*

The characters and events in this book are fictitious; the locale is sketched from life

'Willem II's'. She stuck one between his thick lips and held a match to it. He sucked.

'Happy now?'

'Huh,' he grunted. 'Didn't you talk about some coffee?'

'You've a bloody nerve!' she fired at him.

He smiled again.

'A big cup.'

She didn't be' ... ' ... gain. She went throug' ... 'd to the counter. The large coffee machine was cold but a percolator was bubbling on an electric ring. She took two cups from under the counter, of the size preferred by the truck-drivers, scooped Demarara sugar into them and filled them with the coffee, black. When she returned to the bedroom Teodowicz was still lying on his back. He had his head cradled in his arms and the room was heavy with his cigar-smoke. He sat up to take the cup, blew on it, and drank a big draught; then he set it on the floor and resumed his former position. Wanda re-lit the stubbed cigarette. She sat down on the single, flimsy chair.

'Acting the big man,' she said sourly. 'Tim Teodowicz. The big man.'

He gave his little flicking shrug. He puffed smoke through his wide nostrils.

'I was a big man, once,' he said. 'Back in Poland. Did you know that, Wanda?'

'No,' she said. 'I didn't know it.'

'But I was.' He smiled at nothing. 'I was the mayor of a big town. That seems funny, don't you think? A town as big as Leicester, say. I was the mayor of that town.'

'What was the name of it?' she jeered.

'It doesn't matter, not the name. If I told you, what would that be? A funny name in a funny country. But I was the mayor, and a big man. Lots of money, pretty women. If I did not like a man it went hard with that man.'

5

'And now the big man is a truck driver.'

'Uhuh,' Teodowicz said. He was speaking in his soft, purring tone. He used that tone when he was satisfied. 'Now I own a couple of trucks in a little town in England. Very funny, don't you think? Everything is very funny.'

'Where's Madsen?' Wanda said.

'Ove? He's up in Scotland. A load of machine parts for Glasgow. Are you interested in Ove?'

'He's all right,' she said.

This time Teodowicz directed the smile.

'You like it a lot, don't you?' he said. 'That's all right. It does not worry me. You get a woman who likes it so much, she is usually one you can depend on. And I can depend on you, Wanda. You like the men, but you love me.'

'What makes you so bloody certain of that?'

He waved the cigar. 'I have a knack for it. That is why I am lying here, Wanda, instead of pushing up the daisies. During the war it was not easy for some of us to keep alive, and after the war still harder. But what do you know of that in England? Here, you have never known a war. Oh, it is nice to be English! The government robs you, you rob the government: those are the facts of life in England. Very gentlemanly, very just. I make a very good Englishman.'

She sniffed at the coffee-cup she was nursing, sitting droopingly naked. Her whole body was swearing at him for denying it its rights. Outside on the Road the traffic grumbled and buzzed, never thinning very much till around dawn, and just after. Now it was twenty minutes to twelve. It would go on rolling for four hours more.

'You're a rotten sod, Tim,' she said.

'I know.' The flicking shrug again. 'Sometime you will understand, Wanda. I wanted it badly. It happens at times. You don't know, you are too English; the English are not

6

conditioned as we are. A Polish woman would have understood. Perhaps it is good you are not a Pole.'

'I wouldn't damn well want to be,' she said. 'And you'll never be an Englishman, either.'

The smile came back. 'I am agreeing,' he said. 'I think it may be time I gave up trying.'

'What do you mean?'

'I am going away, Wanda.'

She jerked up straight. 'When?'

'Soon.'

'Where to?'

He stirred lazily, his lids drooping, cat-like.

'I think to America,' he said.

'America! They'd never let you in.'

'I'm not proposing to give them the option.'

'You're mad, Tim. Quite mad.'

He reached for his coffee, drank noisily. 'The reverse,' he said. 'I'm being sane. I have a knack, you remember? It has kept me alive so far.'

'But why? Is it the police?'

'The police!' He chuckled. 'They are my friends. No, your English policemen are wonderful. That is true—oh, so true.'

'Then . . . what?'

The shrug. 'My instinct. I feel I've been here long enough. And you are coming with me, Wanda. That is why I am telling you this.'

'Me—to America?'

'Yes. I will fix it.'

'Man,' she said, 'you're really high.'

He shook his head. 'I am stone cold sober. You are coming with me. We are leaving soon.'

She sat very still on the hard chair, trying to see his eyes in the semi-darkness. And he was watching her too,

7

from his shadows, from under the almost-closed lids.

'I can't,' she said at last. 'This place.'

'I'll appoint an agent to sell it for you,' he said.

'What about your trucks?'

'Madsen can have them.'

'Just like that?'

'I am not entirely impoverished.'

'⟨…⟩,' she said. 'When do we go?'

He sat up, shaking with his low chuckle. 'Soon we go When all is ready. I am playing it by ear, as the Yankees say. So you must be ready, day or night, just to lock those doors and go. You will be discreet, especially with men. You are not to mention my name at all. I will tell you more in a little while. I shall be back quite soon, Wanda.'

He stood up, tall, massive, the hair on his chest dark with sweat. She smelt the odour of his sweat as he reached for the jacket. He put it on, but didn't button it. It was all he wore in the summer. He was a good fifty, perhaps more, but tough as rawhide. And virile.

She gave a moan. 'Don't go yet.'

He took her ⟨…⟩s in his hands and ⟨…⟩ her.

'I shall be back.'

'No. Stay.'

'There are things to be done. I must go.'

'But—do you mean it? This going to America?'

'Have I ever said what I didn't mean?'

'It's so bloody mad,' she groaned.

He was smiling. 'You will see.'

And then he was gone, moving silently, avoiding the close-packed furniture in the next room; vanishing away out of the house while the warmth of his hands was still on her. She sat desolate, listening for the latch-click, but this too was managed silently. All she heard was the buzz of his van as he drove out of the park and towards Offingham. Midnight. She had had

him for exactly an hour. Their loving had lasted, at the most, ten minutes.

'The rotten so-and-so,' she kept murmuring.

Though the room was so warm, her flesh felt chill.

*   *   *

Statement by Robert Arthur Goodings, truck-driver, 42, of Bellingham Crescent, Plaistow, witnessed by Detective-Sergeant Felling, C.I.D., Offingham Constabulary. I left Middlesbrough at 11.10 p.m. on Monday August 12 with a consignment of industrial sulphuric acid for Simper and Parkes of Croydon. I proceeded through Stockton to Darlington and continued down the A1 till I passed the turning to Offingham, which would be at about 4.30 a.m. on Tuesday August 13th. It was beginning to get light, and I thought I would pull up at the lay-by between Offingham and Baddesley for refreshment and a nap. As I came up to it I noticed a green Commer 10-cwt. van already parked there. I pulled in behind it.

*   *   *

Because even the Great Road has its moments of quietness, when the traffic strangely fades, as though an hour had struck which was uncanny for it. It happens at dawn, at the beginning of light, and lasts for a while after sun-up, when the night drivers are resting before the early drivers set out. Then, for a space, the Road is spell-bound in that greyish, brooding light; the bruised surface lies deserted, like a fair-ground when the crowds have gone; sparrows chip along the verges, rattle the paper which wrapped sandwiches; a pheasant may strut in the yellowish field, there is even dew on the dusty hedges. And a solitary car—who is driving now?—scuttles along like a guilty animal, hastening to find a town or village to protect it with their walls.

And Robert Goodings finds a lay-by between Offingham

9

and Baddesley, perhaps the only lay-by on the Road beyond sight and sound of any dwelling. Across the fields, three miles away, rise the pastelled cones of Bintly Power Station; to the south of them, still a long way off, the slant grey roof of an aircraft hanger; up the road, two miles, a drab ribbon called Everham; down the road, out of sight round a bend, a forlorn roadhouse called The Raven. As lonely a spot, as lonely a time as the Great Road can show. When Robert Goodings pulled in his Bedford behind the silent green Commer.

Another bloke taking a spell: that was what Robert Goodings thought. He got down stiffly out of his cab, found a gap in the hedge, relieved himself. Then he stretched his arms, did a knees bend, did some feeble running-on-the-spot; spit a couple of times into the hedge, and climbed back into the cab. He carried a snap-tin and a Thermos. They had both been filled at a caff in Middlesbrough. Tea—the caff made coffee that tasted of mud—and corned-beef sandwiches, larded with mustard. He ate drowsily, thinking of nothing, staring at the back of the green van: glad only to have got to a quiet pull-in after shoving the Bedford all night. But he was noticing, though he wasn't thinking. He was noticing a stain on the concrete by the van. What was the geezer carrying— meat? It looked as though the stuff had begun to drip. He went on eating. He stopped noticing the stain. He noticed the paint-work of the van instead. It had taken a beating, that paint-work had, and there were holes in the panels, too. Holes? His jaw came to a stop. Yes, it was like a blinking sieve. A lot of little round holes punched through it, the paint all cracked away round them. Robert Goodings didn't move for some moments. A car went heedlessly by on the Road.

*   *   *

Report by Detective-Sergeant Felling, C.I.D., Offingham Constabulary. As a result of a telephone call at 5.12 a.m. on

Tuesday August 13th, I proceeded with Detective-Constables Rice and Freeman to the lay-by on the A1 road half a mile north of The Raven roadhouse. I was met there by Robert Arthur Goodings, a truck-driver, who had made the call. I saw there a green Commer 10-cwt. van, Registration Number 525 UAX, the property of Timoshenko Teodowicz, a registered alien residing at 3 Shorters Lane, Offingham, parked in the lay-by. The van was damaged, apparently by extensive fire from an automatic weapon. In the driving seat of the van was the body of a man with multiple bullet wounds. He was aged about fifty, about six feet in height, dark brown hair, pale grey eyes (apparently), and of powerful build. He was wearing a stained khaki jacket without shirt or vest and stained khaki drill trousers. From my personal knowledge I can identify him as Timoshenko Teodowicz, the owner of the van. I have recorded the dead man's fingerprints for comparison with those in the registered alien file (attached).

*   *   *

Statement by Ove Madsen, truck-driver, 39, of 3A Shorters Lane, Offingham, witnessed by Detective-Sergeant Felling, C.I.D., Offingham Constabulary. I am a Naturalized English-man of Norwegian parentage. I am part-owner of the trans-port business which was conducted by the dead man, Timoshenko Teodowicz, whose body I have seen and which I can identify. On Sunday August 11th I left Offingham at 10.45 p.m. with a consignment of electrical parts for John Mackenzie, Clydeside Quay, Glasgow, and I spent the night August 12th–13th at a lodging house at 57 Lockerbie Street, Clydebank (confirmed by Clydebank Cons., D.-S. Felling). I loaded a quantity of strip steel at Govan Mills, Govan and proceeded back to Offingham, arriving at 1 p.m. on Wed-nesday August 14th. I do not own a fire-arm. I do not and have never owned an automatic weapon. I do not and have never owned a Sten gun. I do not know of anybody owning a Sten gun. I do not know who would wish to kill Teodowicz. I do not know that I can benefit in any way by his death. I have to report that Teodowicz was visited on Saturday August 10th, at about 3.30 p.m., at our garage in Shorters Lane, by a man who spoke to him in Polish, and whom he took upstairs into his rooms, and who remained there about 30 minutes. I do not know this man. I did not pay much attention to him, only to him speaking to Teodowicz in Polish. He was about middle height, he was dressed neatly, I think he was wearing sun-glasses. Teodowicz said nothing about him. I think he may have had a limp. I was working at the bench, which is why I did not notice him. He had a quiet, cultivated voice. He was about five feet nine or ten. He may have worn a felt hat. His complexion was pale. I do not think his ears stuck out. I did not notice the cheek-bones. My impression was that he had a cultivated face. My impression was that he was in good circumstances. I did not notice his manner. That is all I know about him.

*   *   *

Medical Report by Police-Surgeon A. S. J. Kermode M.D., M.Ch., Offingham Constabulary. Subject: male deceased delivered to me on the authority of Superintendent Whitaker. Subject aged *c.* 50, 6′1″ in height, in good health, limited adipose tissue. Contents of stomach suggest a meal (eggs, chips, prepared starch, coffee) 4–5 hours before death. Time of death (per r.m.) between 01.00 hrs & 03.00 hrs Tues. Aug. 13th. Cause of death: multiple shot wounds. Extensive wounding of entire system above & including pelvic area on right side. Skull collapsed. Cage of thorax partly collapsed. Extensive damage to bony structure throughout area of wounding, too widespread to detail. Right arm severed above elbow. Left fore-arm variously penetrated. Vital organs, stomach, bowels, extensively damaged. I recovered 67 bullets & counted 92 individual wounds. Should estimate upward of 200 rounds were fired at close range (some signs of powder tattooing, facial tissue recovered & delivered with deceased). Per r.m. deceased was killed where found, or placed there shortly after death. Comment: In 30 years experience, including war service, I have never seen gun-shot injuries such as these. Suggest revenge was clearly the motive, possibly related to some war crime committed by T. in his own country.

*   *   *

Report by Chief Inspector Hallam, Ballistics Dept., New Scotland Yard. Subject: 86 recovered bullets & 193 detonated shells submitted by Offingham Constabulary. Identification: 9 mm. rimless Parabellum pistol cartridge ammunition mfg. by B.S.A. 1944 & 5. Comparison of rifling & breech block marks indicate ammunition fired from Mk. 2 Sten automatic carbine. Ammunition & weapon from service sources, but quantities of these weapons lost, stolen or misappropriated during war.

*   *   *

Interim Report by Detective-Sergeant Felling, C.I.D., Offingham Constabulary. As a result of investigation to date by myself & Detective-Constables Rice & Freeman I have to report that we have obtained no information which might lead to the identification of the murderer of Timoshenko Teodowicz. The search of the premises in Shorters Lane undertaken by us brought to light nothing of significance. We have been unable to find witnesses to testify to seeing anything suspicious in the neighbourhood where the crime was committed, or to hearing shots fired at the relevant time on Aug. 13th. According to Sheila Packman, waitress

13

employed at The Blue Bowl Café, High Street, Offingham, the deceased called there, alone, at about 9.30 p.m., on Aug. 12th, and left when the café closed at 10 p.m., having ordered coffee, driving off in his van in the direction of the A1. We have been unable to find any witness who saw him later than this. We have been unable to trace the man said by Madsen to have visited Teodowicz. We have been unable to trace any connection between Teodowicz and two other men of Polish origin living in this area. We have been unable to trace any friends or intimate acquaintances of Teodowicz who (according to Madsen) lived very much to himself. We have questioned the three women indicated by Madsen as occasionally associating with Teodowicz (Frieda Hixon, Dolly Catchpole, Sybil Wright), but none of them admit having seen him later than Aug. 9th (Dolly Catchpole). We have obtained no information relating to the possession of Sten guns or ammunition. Our investigations show that Teodowicz' transport business, employing two trucks and the van, was legitimate. He ran a current account with the High Street branch of Martin's Bank, average level 3–400 pounds, containing 322 pounds 14 shillings and 7 pence at the time of his death.

*   *   *

Statement by Wanda Christine Lane, Proprietess of The Raven roadhouse, nr. Broadford Turn, Everham, witnessed by Detective-Constable Rice, C.I.D., Offingham Constabulary. The deceased was a customer of mine from time to time. I did not know him except as a customer. I did not see him on the night of Monday August 12th. I think I last saw him on Thursday August 8th at about six p.m. when he pulled in his truck and stopped for a meal. I did not hear any shots fired on the night of August 12th–13th. I had nobody staying overnight on that night. I know the deceased's partner, who is also a customer, but I do not know their friends. They are only customers.

*   *   *

Memo from Sir Clifford Batley, K.B.E., etc., Chief Constable of Offingham, to Superintendent Whitaker. I have read Felling's Interim Report & quite agree that there is no point in holding on, especially with these political implications. I am quite satisfied that we have done the best we can with our resources. Hand it on to the Yard & the Special Branch.

*   *   *

And so it was noticed for a little while, that spot which was otherwise quite anonymous; shown in sketch-maps in newspapers, stared at and stopped at by ten thousand drivers; though it was only one such spot out of the broad centuries of the Road, where death had visited every milestone with its sharp but brief focus. For one dies, but many live, and to live is to forget; who remembers the bludgeoned Celt, the plundered Roman, the stabbed Saxon? Who can show where Rouse murdered or where the masked figure pistolled a farmer? Other days, other deaths, other forgettings; but this the Road. Today a truth concealed in a headline, tomorrow but North and South again.

2

'Right,' Superintendent Empton said. 'Tell me how you know it was Teodowicz. I'm sorry to be bloody-minded, old fellow, but our line of customers tend to be slippery.'

Thursday August 15th. Four of them sitting in Whitaker's office. Three of them heavyweights, Superintendents, and Sergeant Felling, who'd done the field work. Whitaker, the local man, was nervous of the metropolitan talent he'd been sent. He was a large-faced, bronzed and tidy man, mildly paternal, perhaps a little vain. He'd taken to Gently, who sat beside him, and who so far had said very little; but Empton was strictly a foreign type, and obviously made Whitaker feel uneasy. Empton was lean, athletic-looking, vulturine, with eyes like cold blue lamps; in spite of his near-Guards manner he had a predatory air about him. Felling was a hard-eyed C.I.D. man. He was perspiring, but he was not abashed.

'You mean how we knew in the first place, sir—or how we identified the remains?'

'Both, old fellow,' Empton said. 'The one isn't much good without the other.'

Felling opened the file on his knees. 'Here's the Home Office advice note, sir. They informed us that Teodowicz had applied to reside here, March 25th, 'fifty-six. We didn't know of any objections and he took up residence, April 17th.'

'Let me have it.'

Empton took the buff sheet and held it up to the light from the window. Then he scrutinized the printed heading, the typing, the signature and the rubber stamp. Finally he dropped it on the desk.

'Probably genuine,' he said.

'We sent a reply which was acknowledged, sir.'

'No doubt it was.' Empton sounded bored. 'But that hardly means anything. Carry on, Sergeant.'

'Well, sir, he registered with us on April 17th, and all his docs checked with the advice. We made up a card for our R.A. file—this is it, sir. I took his dabs myself. And since then he's reported regularly and never been in any trouble.'

'I'm glad to hear it,' Empton said. 'I'll have the card too, please.' He examined it coldly but perfunctorily, let it drop on the Home Office note. 'And now we come to the interesting part. I've been reading the medical report, old fellow. I notice that the deceased's skull was collapsed and that his right arm was severed. Any comment you care to make?'

Felling was scowling under his sweat. 'The head—that was certainly in a mess, sir—but there was a bit of his face left, on the one side. I've got the photographs here.'

'Thank you.' Empton spread them on the desk. 'Yes . . . you have a good photographer. He brings the point out well.'

'It's the bones, sir,' Felling said thickly. 'The big jawbone and the cheek-bone. If you'd seen the chummie you'd know what I mean. Then there's that skin. Porous and lined.'

'Hmn,' Empton said. 'I see. And this small matter of the arm?'

'It's his all right,' Felling said. 'It matches the other, same all round. Then there's the dabs.'

'Ah yes,' Empton said. He shuffled the photographs together. 'They never lie, do they, old fellow? But we'll just look into them, if you don't mind.'

Felling dived into the file again and produced the card bearing the dead man's prints. Empton tossed it on the pile in front of him, then reached for the brief-case he had stood beside him. It was a beautiful case in natural pigskin. It had a combination lock which he flickered carelessly. From it he took a file marked SECURITY XXX and a morocco-covered box

17

containing a nest of magnifiers. From the file he drew another print record-card, and this he placed by the other two; then, having focused Whitaker's desk-lamp on them, he proceeded with the magnifiers to make a comparison. Felling used the interval to wipe his face, Whitaker watched Empton with concern. Gently was looking mournfully out of the window, where lay the peaceful High Street of Offingham.

'Ah,' said Empton at last, folding the magnifiers. 'I think we're dealing with the one person. You take clear prints, old fellow, both sets are a credit to you.'

'Thank you, sir,' Felling said.

'He's my best man,' Whitaker put in.

'Yes,' Empton said absently. 'I think we can proceed from here.'

He sat back and looked round at them with narrowed, deprecating eyes. Gently turned his gaze from the window. Felling got rid of his handkerchief.

'Perhaps it will help,' Empton continued, 'if I laid some of our cards on the table. Most of this is Top Security, naturally, but I think a run-over can do no harm. If I give you the background it will help you to distinguish some of the nuances you may have overlooked. But I must make it crystal clear that none of this is to go any further.'

'Of course, of course,' Whitaker said.

'Yes,' Empton said. 'Then here are some facts. Timoshenko Teodowicz is a political refugee who arrived in this country in 1947. He was born in Grodz, in eastern Poland, in or about 1910. During the last war he was a petty black marketeer and kept on the windy side of the Germans. He was denominated a war criminal by the Russians and was obliged to disappear, and he eventually turned up in the British Zone of Germany in January 1947. His case was investigated and appeared genuine, as far as the particulars went. He was probably a rogue, but not a war criminal within our meaning of the term. So he was admitted as an R.A. in November 1947, and to the best of our knowledge he has not abused the privilege. He resided in Leeds, Birmingham and Leicester before he applied to live here. He was a builder's labourer for two years, drove a truck for Great Universal for three years. This would appear to be what we know about Timoshenko Teodowicz.'

Whitaker shuffled. 'Appears to be?'

'I wouldn't', said Empton, 'put it higher.'

'But didn't you say his case was investigated?'

'I did say that,' Empton said. 'It was investigated, it bore out his story. Teodowicz of Grodz was a real person. But I'm afraid it means very little, old man—we take these things with a grain of salt.'

'Then who do you think he was?'

Empton's teeth showed briefly. 'Almost anyone. One of theirs, a free-lance, perhaps the veritable Teodowicz. The refugee traffic is much favoured for the planting of agents. When we find one we buy him or use him—only an occasional amateur makes the headlines.'

'But what use would an agent be in Offingham?'

'None at all, I should imagine. But Teodowicz wasn't tied to Offingham. His trucking took him wherever he chose.'

A pause. Gently had taken out his pipe and was sucking it, cold and empty. The sound appeared to irritate Empton, who threw him a quick, chill glance. Whitaker's expression was unconvinced; his eyes wandered about the documents on the desk. Empton dipped into his file again and came out with a quarter-plate photograph.

'Now. We come to the aspect which to us is the key factor. You have evidence to show that Teodowicz was visited a short time before his death. This is a classic pattern with us, one which occurs in case after case. A man is visited by a foreign-spoken stranger, and shortly afterwards, he dies. The newspaper gentry, of course, jump to certain conclusions, but between you and me they are usually wide of the mark. Refugees are certainly pressured to return to their own country, but we know of no clear instance of assassination following a refusal. What the pattern usually indicates is a flagrant double-cross. The victim is an agent who is playing double and who refuses to toe the line. His visitor brings him an ultimatum—the terms are naturally a little harsh—and the agent is reluctant; it may then be necessary to liquidate him.'

Whitaker screwed up his eyes. 'You mean it really goes on, this sort of thing?'

Empton showed his teeth again. 'But of course it does, old man. Jungle law and all that. You can't have intelligence without it. If a man is a threat to security and you can't buy him or coerce him, you have to kill him: that's logic. We live in a split world, you know. Now if this is what has happened to your man, and I'm presuming that it is, then I'm afraid we'll never get a conviction in the case. I can probably trace the killer and cause him to return from where he came, but that's as far as it will go. A trial may not be expedient.'

Whitaker turned to Gently, as though seeking support. Gently kept sucking his pipe and staring glumly at nothing.

'But, look here—' Whitaker began.

'I know, I know,' Empton interrupted. 'British justice and all that—mustn't give the myth a knock.'

'But it amounts to condoning a murder.'

'Exactly that,' Empton said. 'I'm sorry. We're doing it every day. I'm sure the novelty will soon wear off with you.'

He tapped the photograph he had brought.

'This', he said, 'could be our man. Jan Kasimir, thirty-nine, late of Krackow, Poland. Another refugee, naturally—he's been in England for two years—getting acclimatized, you might say, and establishing the innocence of his character. He resides in Hampstead where he works for an instrument-maker and behaves like a model alien. We've kept our usual discreet eye on him. He was about ripe for a commission.'

He pushed the photograph across to Whitaker. It showed a good-looking man with sharp-cut features. He had dark hair, dark eyes, a tooth-brush moustache and a delicate chin. He was wearing a plain bow tie and was facing the camera with confidence.

'How do you know this is him?' Whitaker asked.

'I don't know,' Empton said. 'I'm following my nose, old man. I want this photograph shown to Madsen. The description he gave is pretty sketchy, but such as it is it fits Kasimir. And Kasimir limps, that's the point. I read of the limp and remembered Kasimir.'

Gently removed his pipe, and coughed. *A62033*

'Is a question in order?' he asked.

Empton flickered a look at him. 'Of course,' he said. 'Fire away.'

'Do you know that Teodowicz was an agent?'

'No.'

'But you would have done—if he were playing double?'

Empton showed his teeth precisely. 'Nicely taken, old man,' he said.

'It naturally occurred to me,' Gently said. 'The line you're taking seems to rest on it.'

'It does indeed,' Empton said. 'On that, and the rather familiar pattern. No, we don't know he was an agent, and he had not made any approach to us. But he may have been meditating an approach, and was perhaps killed for that reason.'

'I see,' Gently said.

'And the pattern remains,' said Empton.

'Yes, the pattern,' Gently said.

Empton didn't say anything.

'One other thing,' Gently said. 'Is the way he was killed quite typical? I don't meet this sort of thing very often, and I thought the number of bullets impressive.'

'Perhaps unusual,' Empton said.

'Less than good professional standard?'

'It depends on the purpose,' Empton said. 'We may find a reason for it later.'

'Two hundred bullets,' Gently said. 'Where one would have served the same purpose. An overall burst of about forty seconds. Scything the victim up and down.'

'That's what struck us,' Whitaker said. 'We felt certain it was a case of a revenge killing. Or the work of a maniac, one or the other. Nobody could be sane to do that.'

Empton lifted one eyebrow. 'Thank you,' he said, 'for your reactions. But agents are liquidated in various ways, according to the exigencies of the moment. I agree that this instance looks unprofessional. I thought at first it was to conceal identity. But I have no doubt it was done for a purpose other than emotional catharsis.'

'I'm not so sure,' Whitaker said.

'Yes,' Empton said. 'Is Madsen handy?'

'He's been waiting since ten,' Whitaker said.

'Right,' Empton said. 'Have him in.'

*   *   *

Felling fetched Madsen in. He was a pale-haired Scandinavian who kept nervously smiling. He had a long straight nose, a girlish mouth and fair complexion, but his frame was bony and solid and he walked with a springing step. He was given a chair by the desk, and sat it awkwardly, stooping forward. He smiled at Gently and Whitaker. The smile drooped when it came to Empton. Empton stared at him, apparently casual. But the smile faded right away.

'So you're Madsen,' Empton said. 'Come from Bekkestua, don't you?'

'Yes,' Madsen said. 'Bekkestua.'

'Skansenveien.'

'Yes, Skansenveien.'

'Number twenty-two,' Empton said.

'Yes, number twenty-two,' Madsen said.

'A nice place to live,' Empton said. 'Why didn't you go back there, Madsen?'

Madsen tried to make his smile. It ended up in a twitch.

'My people,' he said. 'They are all dead. My father was shot by the Germans. My mother, my sister, my fiancée . . . there is nothing to go back to. The house was burned to the ground. I went back once, to make my claim.'

'Touching,' Empton said. 'The claim was thirty thousand kroner.'

'It is about fifteen hundred pounds.'

'Hardly worth claiming,' Empton said.

Madsen tried the smile again, but it just wouldn't come. He moved his hands inside his knees; big, powerful-looking hands.

'What is it you want?' he said suddenly. 'There is nothing I try to hide. I am a Norwegian by birth, that is so, I don' make any secret of this.'

'Just as well,' Empton said. 'We know all about you, Madsen.'

'But what do you know? I do not mind!'

Empton said: 'We've been talking to Kasimir.'

Madsen's eyes were tugged to him, flinched, fell away again. Empton sat in a lazy poise, his eyes lazy. But unblinking.

'Who—who is that?' Madsen asked.

'The one they sent here. Who brought the terms.'

'I do not know what you mean.'

'Oh yes you do. Kasimir talked.'

'But I do not know any Kasimir—this is double-dutch, about Kasimir!'

'Stop acting innocent,' Empton said. 'It's a waste of time. We know what you did.'

Madsen was trembling. He smiled at the desk, at Gently, at Whitaker, at the desk again. Gently was sitting hunched and expressionless. Whitaker was frowning. Felling stood by the door. Madsen lifted his big hands.

'I tell you, I know nothing,' he said. 'I have never heard of a man, Kasimir. What you are saying doesn't mean anything.'

'Oh, forget the act,' Empton said. 'If you play ball, you won't get hurt. We're calling the tricks now, Madsen, you'd better get that fixed in your head. Who's the contact?'

'I don' know—'

'Answer the question!'

'I tell you—'

'You'll tell us a lot of lies, no doubt.'

'It is the truth—I just don' know!'

'Very well then,' Empton said. 'Play it your way if you like, Madsen. Teodowicz made the same mistake. An operator only makes it once.'

'I'm telling you everything!' Madsen cried. 'I am trying to help. What else can I do? You ask me these questions which don' mean nothing, what can I say? I didn' kill Tim!'

'But you know who did,' Empton said.

'I don'. I was not anywhere here.'

'You were in the garage when the man walked in.'

'The garage?' Madsen stared a moment. 'I saw that man, yes, I said so—I tell you everything I know about that man. All the questions I answer about him. And it is true—he did come in.'

'Oh, he came in all right,' Empton said. 'And you know his name, don't you, Madsen?'

'But I did not speak to him at all!'

Empton let his teeth show.

'Let's see how truthful you are,' he said. 'I've got a test for you here, Madsen. The man you know about is in this stack

24

of photographs. We know which one—now let's see if you do.'

He handed the photographs over the desk. Madsen took them from him uncertainly. He raised his eyes to look at Empton, dropped them quickly, began to fumble the photographs. Empton's eyes stayed fixed on Madsen's face. Madsen's fingers were big and clumsy. The photographs showed a number of men who appeared to be of un-English extraction.

'Take your time, Madsen,' Empton said. 'You may find some other friends of yours.'

'No,' Madsen said. 'I don' know them. I don' know any of these men.'

'You surprise me,' Empton said. 'Don't you have any friends, Madsen?'

'I've got some friends,' Madsen said.

'Well, well,' Empton said softly.

Madsen came to the end of the stack.

'It isn' no good,' he said. 'I don' know them.'

'Can't you have a stab at it?' Empton said. 'Look better that way, wouldn't it, Madsen?'

'I didn' see that man properly,' Madsen said.

'Couldn't you take a chance?' Empton said.

Madsen laid the stack on the desk. His mouth was tight, turned down at the corners.

'Perhaps I made a mistake,' Empton said. 'Perhaps he wasn't in that pack after all, Madsen. Maybe he's still back here in the envelope. I'll play the cards. You call.'

He picked up the envelope the pack had come from, took out another photograph, threw it on the desk. Madsen eyed it, made no motion. Empton threw down another, and another. Then he stopped. Madsen had bent forward. The Kasimir photograph had appeared.

'Your call,' Empton murmured.

'That one,' Madsen said. 'Perhaps that could be him.'

*   *   *

Empton smoked: a straw-coloured tube containing a grey and pungent tobacco; leaning far back in his chair and letting the smoke arise from his mouth. He took no notice while Gently was putting his few routine questions to Madsen. He had packed his papers in the brief-case and stood the case on the desk. Whitaker, on the other hand, was giving his attention to the questions. He had his back half-turned to Empton as though the better to observe the interchange. Felling continued by the door. He was also watching and listening keenly.

'How long had you known Teodowicz?' Gently asked.

Madsen's smiles were beginning to return. They were not deliberate, not insincere, but seemed to well up in him like a sunny child's. You looked at him, spoke to him, and he smiled.

'It will be over six years, I think, now. . . . I knew him when he drove for Gus, then I used to meet him on the road. And when I told him about my money he said, buy a truck and join him here. So that is what I did with my money, and we have a ver' good business.'

'You were good friends with him?'

'Oh, yes. Good friends.'

'You spent your free time together?'

'Yes, when we were off together. But I am in Plymouth sometimes, say, and he is in Norwich or Glasgow, like that. We do not see ver' much of each other, just in the week-ends, perhaps.'

'What did you do when you were off together?'

'Oh, we have a drink, have a meal. Go to the pictures, pick up two women. We don' do anything ver' special.'

'Was Teodowicz fond of women?'

'Oh, yes, he liked the women. Wherever he goes he pick one up . . . you know. Not particular.'

'But wasn't there one special woman?'

'No, Tim liked them all. He only want the one thing from them—then mm, mm! Goodbye.'

'What about men. Did he mix with them?'

'Oh, other drivers he talk to.'

'Did he have any special men friends?'

'No, he like the ladies best.'

'Did he have any men friends at all?'

Madsen thought. 'No, not really friends. I don' think he get on so well with the men. He don' talk so much, don' laugh and joke.'

'No Polish friends he used to see?'

'No, he would not talk to a Pole. He say he want to forget Poland, he is ver' unhappy back there.'

'Did he talk about that?'

'He tell me they would hang him if he went back. Something he did in the war-time, selling things. You know.'

'Anything else?'

'No, nothing else.'

'Not about them trying to make him go back?'

'Nothing about that at all. He never talk about himself much.'

'After this man had been to visit him—didn't you ask him what it was about? You were partners, and good friends. Surely something must have been said.'

Madsen's smiling was embarrassed. 'Yes . . . you know . . . I do mention it. Tim wouldn' speak to a Pole as a rule, this one he take upstairs and have a chat with. So I mention something.'

'What did he say?'

'Oh, he say forget about it. It was just somebody passing through who stop by for a chat.'

'Did that square with what you saw of him?'

Again the embarrassment. 'I don' know. . . . At first he seem nervous, speak ver' low . . . and Tim don' say anything for a moment.'

'Then?'

'Then Tim give a shrug, say something quick to him in Polish. Then they go out of the garage and I hear them go up the steps to the flat.'

'What happened when they came down?

'Oh, nothing at all. They are not saying anything. This man go straight out of the garage and Tim, he get out a cigar and light it.'

'Do you know who wanted to kill Tim, Madsen?'

'No. I don' have any idea.

'Was he never in trouble over his women?'

'No. They are prostitutes. You know?'

Gently sucked some more on the empty pipe. Empton drove smoke towards the ceiling. His legs were stretched out by the desk, an expensive brogue by an expensive brogue. The street below was stirring a little. The clock said ten minutes to one. Felling appeared to be still perspiring, since he had just wiped his face again.

Gently said: 'Have you any knowledge that Teodowicz was engaged in espionage?'

'Esp'nage?' Madsen looked puzzled.

'That he was a spy, selling secret information.'

'A spy? Oh, no . . . that is ver' ridiculous! You cannot be thinking Tim was a spy.'

'What makes you so positive?'

'It is so unlikely! You do not know Tim at all. He is—what do you say? He want to forget it, to turn his back, to live quiet on his own. He don' want to be mixed up with anything like that, it is ver' ridiculous. You do not know him.'

'Ha, ha,' Empton said.

'But yes, it is true,' Madsen said. 'He have all this trouble back in Poland, now he just want to live quiet.'

'And that was your picture of him,' Gently said. 'Now he just wanted to live quiet.'

28

'But yes. It is the same all the time I know him.'

'Thank you,' Gently said. 'That's all for the moment.'

★   ★   ★

The door closed.

Empton got up, stubbed the cigarette, flexed his hands.

'Probably genuine,' he said. 'Lacked the *savoir-faire* of a professional. Teodowicz strung him along nicely with his I-want-to-be-alone act. Teodowicz was probably a useful man. A pity he put a foot wrong.'

'I don't know,' Whitaker said. 'I'm still as puzzled as I was before. There doesn't seem anything to get a hold on, it's shuttered up all round.'

Empton's teeth. 'We're used to it, old man. It's the view these cases always present. You get a murder happening out of the blue, no motive, no angles. Then you know what you're up against and you begin to look in certain directions. The real break has been that limp. Your man did well to get Madsen to remember it.'

'Felling's my best man,' Whitaker said. 'But what do you want us to do now?'

'Nothing whatever,' Empton said. 'There's nothing further you can do. I'll go back to town and pick up Kasimir and apply various forms of pressure. Then we will decide what we will decide. Some results may appear in the morning paper.'

'Well,' Whitaker said, 'it's beyond me. And you apparently know how to handle it.'

'Leave it at that,' Empton said. 'As of now it's our pigeon.'

He took hold of the brief-case. He looked squarely at Gently.

'And what's your theory, old man,' he asked.

Gently shrugged. 'I don't have a theory. I'm only here to make up the party.'

'You still think it's one of your amateur killings?'

'I'm only at the stage of collecting facts.'

'It'll be a labour of love, old man, I think.'

'Taxpayers' money,' Gently said.

Empton's teeth. Then he shook hands. He had a curiously unsubstantial grasp. Whitaker went with him down the stairs and stood a moment chatting in the doorway. Gently rose and moved over to the window. He saw Empton walk swingingly across to his car. It was a Jaguar coupé enamelled red and probably of a mark number known to the enthusiast. Empton slid into it and surged away. Whitaker came back up the stairs. Gently moved back to the desk to reclaim his pipe and his trilby.

'Are you driving back too?' Whitaker asked.

Gently shook his head. 'Just going to lunch. I'd like to have Felling show me round this afternoon—unless you have a back-log of amateur crimes.'

Whitaker chuckled. 'No. You can have him. I just wondered if you thought it worthwhile to stay.'

'Purely routine,' Gently said. 'And probably idle curiosity.'

Whitaker said: 'I can't get over that fellow. Are they all like that in the Special Branch?'

'A few.' Gently sucked his pipe. 'It's a split world,' he said.

3

OFFINGHAM, Offgms. (A.S. Offa & *ham*, home). 16,129. Map 12 C5. Mkt. Sat. E.C. Weds. London 52¼, Northampton 37¼, Bedford 19½, Leicester 57. 1 mile E. of A1. On R. Ound, crossed here by Med. bridge of 12 arches. Church St. Lawrence Perp., carved oak roof; also St. Olaf, Dec., traces of fan vaulting, painted screen. Traces of 12th c. priory near R. Med. house in Mkt. Pl. Inds: printing, furniture mfg., light elec. products. Centre of a considerable Agri. area & county town of Offgms.

*   *   *

Gently took Felling to lunch with him at Fullton's Restaurant in the Market Place. The dining-room was on the first floor and looked across market stalls to St. Lawrence's. At lunchtime Offingham came out of its trance; in its small-town way it looked crowded. The pavements were busy. In the Market Place people stood eating fish-and-chips out of newspapers. Clerks, shopkeepers, businessmen crowded the tables in the restaurants. There was little motion of traffic. All the shops had their doors locked. A communal atmosphere pervaded the town; everyone turned out for lunch.

Gently ordered a mixed grill, Felling a modestly priced chop. At a word from Felling they had been found a secluded table at the very end of the range of windows. Gently said nothing until he had eaten and the sergeant took his cue from Gently. Felling was around forty. He was dark, had a ruddy complexion and humourless good-looks. He watched Gently as they ate. Gently looked out of the window. They had both ordered iced lager and it went down very well.

At the coffee Gently said: 'Have you any ideas you haven't put on record?'

Felling looked up sharply from his coffee, then back to it again.

'What makes you say that, sir?' he asked.

'You've done the field work,' Gently said. 'You put into a report what you're sure of. But you get hunches, too. It's hunches I'm after.'

'Don't know if I've got any,' Felling said. 'It's like the Super put it, it's all shuttered up. There's only Madsen you could really suspect, and he just wasn't here. You can't get round it.'

'He couldn't have worked it?' Gently asked.

Felling shook his head positively. 'Not unless he's got a double sir. I gave the Clydebank lot a minute description. Then there's the woman at the lodgings, sir—Madsen was a regular when he was that way. And they knew him at Mackenzie's and the Govan Mills. He was the only prospect. I chased him hard.'

'What was Teodowicz doing over the week-end?'

Felling twisted his mouth. 'I wish I knew, sir. According to Madsen he was in the garage part of Sunday, messing about with his van or something. Madsen saw him last at tea-time. He was gone when Madsen came for his truck.'

'Where was he in the morning?'

'Madsen doesn't know, sir. He was lying in to get his sleep up. He was driving on the night Friday–Saturday and was out on the booze Saturday night. He went round to the Blue Bowl to have his lunch, and when he came back, Teodowicz was in the garage.'

'And Monday?'

Felling turned over his hand. 'A blank, till he went into the Blue Bowl. I can't even find where he had that meal. He only had coffee at the Blue Bowl.'

'Yes . . . coffee. What was that meal again?'

'Egg and chips. And perhaps some sort of gateaux.'

'A café meal,' Gently said.

'But not from any café in Offingham, sir.'

Gently drank some of his coffee, his eye wandering to St. Lawrence's. 'According to the medical report,' he said, 'the meal was eaten at eight p.m. at the earliest. Probably later, say nine p.m. And at nine-thirty he's in the Blue Bowl drinking coffee. He would have eaten that meal not far away . . . it sounds like a transport café meal.'

'Yes sir, it does,' Felling said.

'Which suggests a journey,' Gently said. 'He may have been some distance away from Offingham—he may have left on the Sunday evening. That would account for his absence on Monday, why you can't find trace of him here.'

'Yes sir . . . could be,' Felling said.

'You're thinking otherwise?' Gently asked.

'No sir.' Felling's head shook again. 'I was still trying to place that café, sir.'

'It'll probably be on the A1.'

'Yes sir. Could be on the Bedford road. But if it's only half-an-hour's drive, sir, that doesn't leave much of a choice. Going north there's a place at Syleham, and south there's The Raven, near where he was killed. But Rice has checked The Raven for me, sir. Teodowicz hadn't been seen there since last Thursday.'

'It might be further off,' Gently said. 'An hour and a half is the outside limit. Perhaps you'd care to continue the check.'

'Yes sir, I'll do that,' Felling said.

'Also,' Gently said, 'there's the matter of the gun.'

Felling looked blank. 'That's a dead end, sir. We've checked around until we're dizzy. I reckon the chummie imported it, sir.'

'From service sources, the report says. Have you got any barracks near here?'

'Not nearer than Bedford,' Felling said.

'An aerodrome?'

Felling hesitated. 'There's Great Grimston and Barton Novers. And Huxford, that's still being used.'

'Which is the nearest?'

'Well . . . Huxford. But it's only a maintenance unit, sir. It was an airfield they ran up during the war. They've been talking of closing it for years.'

'Where does it lie?'

'Nearer Baddesley, sir.'

'How far away from the A1?'

'A couple of miles . . .'

'How far from the lay-by where Teodowicz was killed?'

'Maybe three,' Felling said. 'Across the fields, that is.'

'Mmn,' Gently said. 'That's interesting. It might bear looking into. Or have you checked there already?'

Felling chewed his lip. 'No.' he said.

*   *   *

The shops opened again and once more the streets were nearly empty. A few housewives with baskets and prams, some pensioners loitering, a little through traffic. A mile away the A1 rolled its ceaseless pageant of commerce. Under four of its bridge's twelve arches the weedy Ound stole greenly along. The air was warm and quite still. The sky was hazy, greyish-white.

Felling led Gently across the Market Place and into a street which left it at the corner. It was a street of withdrawn yellow-brick houses, their walls flush to the pavement. Half-way along was a Methodist chapel with polished, liver-coloured columns, reminding the passer-by from its notice board that God was not Mocked. The street was a cul-de-sac.

34

Felling branched to the left into a more dilapidated street. It was bordered by a scrap yard, a carpenter's shop, a shambles exhaling disinfectant, a garage and warehouse of a wholesale fruiterer, some lock-up garages and tarred brick walls. This was also a cul-de-sac but a lane led off by the garages. The lane was enclosed by the same tarred walls, from over which peered nettles and willow-herb. The lane twisted to the left, broadened out into a small court, continued beyond it by ramshackle buildings to an unexpected glimpse of pollard willows. Felling stopped when they came to the court.

'This is Teodowicz' place,' he said.

At the side of the court was an old building of yellow brick into the front of which had been let folding doors. There were small sash windows above the doors and on the right a gateway leading into a yard. From the yard a wooden stairway slanted up the wall to a landing and door on the first floor. On the opposite side of the yard was a two-storey outbuilding with a similar stairway. The yard was filled with junk and nettles and there was no sign-board. The place looked faceless.

'Teodowicz lived over the garage,' Felling said. 'Madsen lives across the yard. There's nobody else in Shorters Lane. That's what made it so difficult to check his movements.'

'Quite a hideout,' Gently said.

'Yes sir.' Felling shot him a look.

'Where does the lane go, away from here?'

'It joins the road by the river, sir.'

'Are there any other ways in and out?'

'Yes sir. There's an alley at the rear of the building. And there are plenty of bolt-holes through these old yards—you can work through to Skinner Street and the market.'

'Very convenient,' Gently said. 'Mr. Teodowicz had a provident nature.'

Felling crossed to the folding doors, in which was included

35

an entry, produced a tagged bunch of keys and unlocked the latter. He peered inside, stepped over the threshold. Gently followed him in. The tall radiator of a Leyland truck rose in the sweet-smelling gloom inside the entry. Some light leaked in through two high small windows, but the splash from the entry seemed to dazzle it. Felling moved to his right and found some switches. Three cobwebbed bulbs turned yellow above them.

Two trucks, both Leylands, of slightly differing models. They were each painted dark green and bore no form of trade lettering. They stood gigantically in the small garage and left little room either side, but behind them ran an oil-soaked bench with a vice and tools on racks above it. Under the bench lay old tyres and tubes and a variety of oil-stained rubbish. To the left of the bench stood a tall metal cabinet, green and oily, its door sagging open. A drip-tray and pails stood about, all containing drained oil. On the bench were two oil-stained mugs. One of them contained tea-dregs.

'He kept the van out in the yard,' Felling said, pointing to a side-door. 'That'll be the plastic cover for it. I've seen it parked out there.'

'You've been after him before?' Gently asked.

'Once,' Felling said. 'It was nothing. He'd been on a trip up to Fraserburgh and forgot to punch the clock with us.'

Gently moved over to the cabinet, pushed the door open wider. Its shelves were stuffed with a medley of spares, plugs, gaskets, lamps, tape. On the bottom shelf was an old box-file lying with some manufacturer's literature. Gently pushed the flap open. It contained a list of tyre prices.

'Where's his office?'

Felling stared. 'Don't think he had an office, sir.'

'He had to keep records and accounts. You took a look at them, didn't you?'

'Yes sir, of course,' Felling said. 'They're in the drawer of

36

a table upstairs. A bit sketchy, they were, sir. I couldn't get anything out of them.'

Gently grunted, left the cabinet, went round to the cabs of the trucks.

'Which is his?'

Felling pointed to the older one. Gently put his foot on the step and hoisted himself up. Inside the cab was roomy and bare with the engine casing between the two seats. On the driving seat lay a raw slab of Dunlopillo, on the other a black P.V.C. jacket. In the panel-locker were a couple of old *Reveilles* and a paper-back novel by Hank Jansen. A khaki-coloured canvas bag hung between the two seats. It contained an unwashed Thermos, an empty aluminium sandwich-tin.

'Where's his log-book?' Gently asked.

'I took it upstairs, sir,' Felling said. 'I thought it had better be with the other stuff than knocking about down here.'

'When did he make his last trip?'

Felling hesitated. 'It would be mid-week, sir. He spent the Friday night with one of the pros, and he was seen at The Raven with his truck at six p.m. on Thursday. I reckon he'd have been coming back off a trip.'

'You haven't checked with the log-book entry?'

'No sir, I haven't.' Felling looked hard at the truck. 'It didn't occur to me to do that, sir.'

'Mmn,' Gently said. 'I think we'll do that now. An analysis of that log-book may be interesting.'

'Yes sir,' Felling said flatly. 'I'm sorry, sir. This business took us all a bit by surprise.'

Gently climbed down again and Felling went to unlock the side-door. In the yard opposite to it was a bare patch where the van had been used to stand. The upper door of the outbuilding stood ajar and the two windows were open, and at one Madsen's face appeared momentarily, staring down at the two policemen. It vanished quickly. As they mounted the stairway the door opposite slowly closed. Felling unlocked the door on their side. He stood back. Gently entered.

The door opened directly into a scullery with a sink, a dresser and an old gas stove; very bare and neglected and smelling of grease and gas. From it a door led through to a second room containing a bed and some furniture, and beyond it was a third room, empty, but with a corner panelled off and containing a water-closet. The bed was an army pattern iron bedstead made up with blankets and a soiled pillow. The chairs were of the folding varnished-wood sort used in messes and canteens. A green metal locker, resembling the garage cabinet, took the place of a wardrobe. The table was a plain kitchen table. On the walls were taped pin-up pictures.

'Not much of a dive, sir,' Felling said, coming into the room behind Gently. 'More like a war-time billet. He was used to rough-living, I reckon.'

'Yet he was making money,' Gently said.

'Yes sir. His current account showed that. And the tax people let on he was showing a fair-size return.'

'So what was he spending it on?'

Felling shrugged. 'Wouldn't know, sir,' he said. 'Perhaps he's got a hoard somewhere—putting it away for his old age. He used to draw cash from the bank, except for bills on the truck. He'd got about twenty nicker in his pocket. As far as we could put the bits together.'

'Let's take a look at those accounts.'

Felling went to the table. He opened the drawer, looked in. He stood still staring into it.

'Well,' Gently said.

Felling was reddening. 'The bloody devil!' he said. 'They've gone.'

He pulled the drawer right out. It contained a pin-up and an old safety-razor.

*　　　*　　　*

'One of your men wouldn't have removed them?'

Felling shook his head angrily. 'Not without telling me they wouldn't. I'm damned certain they haven't been here.'

'When were you here last?' Gently asked.

'Yesterday morning—and the stuff was here then. That's when I fetched the log-book up. And I've had the keys all the time!'

He still kept glaring at the drawer as though unable to believe it vacant. The face in the pin-up wore a broad smile; the edges of the sheet showed signs of taping.

'Was that picture in there yesterday?'

'Picture . . . ? No, it ruddy well wasn't!'

'Does that suggest anything to you?'

'Only that somebody's taking the mike.'

Gently shrugged, turned to look at the walls. There were twenty-four of the pin-up pictures. They were arranged without method round the room, but a space marked by tape showed where a twenty-fifth had been. And the twenty-four on the walls differed from the one in the drawer. They stared down passionately, coyly, but they did not have smiles.

'Had Madsen a key?'

'Madsen . . . of course!'

'But had he a key?'

'He said he hadn't. The liar.'

'Was that paper ash in the grate the last time you were here?'

'Paper ash . . . ?'

Felling turned to scowl at the grate. It contained a pile of stirred grey-black ash, much of which had fallen through into the pan. A few scorched corners of sheets appeared amongst it, also a piece of cardboard bearing a shrivelled grey deposit. Felling swooped on the latter.

'That's the log-book cover. It had one of those bindings which they tell you are weather-proof.'

39

'And these'll be the accounts that have gone up with it.'

'The devil!' Felling said. 'What sort of game is he playing?'

'I think we'd better ask him,' Gently said.

'I'd like to kick his behind for him,' Felling said. 'There's just no reason for burning this stuff.'

'Fetch him up,' Gently said. 'We'll see.'

Felling went. Gently stared at the grate, at the poker which stood there. He picked up a piece of kindling, stirred the ashes afresh. The burning had been carried out thoroughly and he could find no significant fragments. The ashes were cold. The burning had taken place probably about twelve hours earlier. The only fragment of any size was the piece of the log-book cover. He left the grate and went to the door and examined the lock and the door-jamb; then to the sash windows, each of which were bolted, unbolting them and inspecting them outside and in. He found no marks that were suggestive. He stood looking about the rooms. Along with the smells of grease and gas was the grubby smell of dry rot. He looked in the locker. Some seedy clothes. He entered the toilet. A Sunday newspaper. In the dresser in the scullery were some scraps of food, crockery, cutlery, utensils, a clean towel. Under a cup an unpaid electricity bill. It was the only document in the place.

A scuffling and tramping on the stairway: Felling had returned, shoving Madsen in front of him. The Norwegian looked flustered, his colour coming and going, his smiles chasing each other as though he had a nervous complaint.

'Here he is, sir,' Felling said grimly. 'And he admits it was him who burned that stuff.'

'I didn't know,' Madsen said. 'I'm ver' sorry.' He smiled unceasingly and writhed his hands.

'You'd better sit down,' Gently said.

Madsen sat. Felling folded his arms, stared at Madsen

thunderously. Gently sat too. He took his pipe out and filled it. He lit the pipe. He looked at Madsen.

'Go on,' he said. 'Tell me about it.'

'I don' know,' Madsen said. 'I just did it.'

'When did you do it?'

'Oh . . . yesterday I do it.'

'When yesterday?'

'I . . . it was in the evening.'

'What time in the evening?'

'Oh . . . it was late. When I come in from the pub . . . you know?'

'Eleven? Twelve?'

'Maybe about then.'

'About when?'

'About eleven . . . say a half past eleven.'

'Not half-past twelve?'

'No . . . I don' know. It is earlier maybe . . . perhaps later.'

'Why did you break in when you had a key?'

'I . . . ' Madsen stumbled. He threw a smile at Felling. 'I think, perhaps, possibly . . . '

'He had a key!' Felling snapped. 'He told me he hadn't, but he had. Now he say's he's thrown it away.'

'Did you have a key?' Gently asked.

'Yes,' Madsen said, 'a key, yes. I forget it when I am asked . . . then I think I'd better throw it away.'

'Why?'

Madsen's smile was freezing. 'It is . . . because I say I haven' one.'

'Couldn't you have hidden it?'

'Yes . . . perhaps. . . . '

'Yet you threw it away?'

Madsen said nothing.

'Right,' Gently said. 'You had a key. You could get into

this flat at any time. Why did you come here late last night instead of earlier on—say the afternoon?'

'But I am not here then,' Madsen said.

'We had him till six,' Felling said. 'Making a statement.'

'But yes,' Madsen said. 'Making the statement. Then I go for a meal, go to the pub.'

'You spent the evening in a pub?'

'Oh, yes. At the Marquis of Gransby.'

'When you'd just had the shock of hearing about your partner?'

'Drinking it off,' Felling put in scornfully.

Madsen smiled and trembled. 'Yes, that is it. I have the shock, I go for a drink. I am just come back from driving all night when I hear this thing. I go for the drink.'

'Let's get this straight,' Gently said. 'You were tired with driving. You'd had a shock. You'd been questioned for some hours by the police. Then you go to a pub to be questioned over again. Or were you a stranger in the Marquis of Gransby?'

'No,' Madsen said. 'I was not a stranger.'

'Wouldn't you have wanted to be on your own?'

'I don' know,' Madsen said. 'It is the shock.'

'So you spend the evening being questioned by your friends.'

'I don' know,' Madsen said. 'That is how it is.'

Gently puffed. 'All right,' he said. 'Let's carry it on from there. The pub turned out, you came back here. Tell me what you did next.'

'I come up here next,' Madsen said.

'Why?'

'These things . . . I am going to burn them.'

'Why did you want to burn them?'

'Because . . . perhaps. . . .' Madsen licked his lips, moved his hands. 'It is hard to tell. I am ver' upset . . . the head in a

42

whirl, you know? I think that Tim would like this done. I think he will want me to do it.'

'Why would Tim want it done?'

'I don' know . . . this is what I think. I am ver' tired, I have been drinking. I think that Tim is there with me. . . .'

'Go on.'

'Yes, I come up the stairs, and go in and burn those papers. It seems the right thing, you know? I burn them up in the grate.'

'Where were the papers you burned?'

'In here . . . in this drawer.'

'Why didn't you burn Tim's log-book, too?'

'The log-book . . . ? That would be . . . I don't know.'

'You don't know if you burned the log-book?'

'Yes . . . my head, it is not ver' clear. . . .'

'Did you burn it?'

'I burn everything . . . all there is in the drawer.'

'His memory's failing,' Felling said. 'He told me he'd burned the log-book.'

'Yes, the log-book,' Madsen said. 'The account-book, the log-book.'

'So,' Gently said, 'you burned them. You put a match to them, and they burned.'

'Yes, I wait while they burn. I think Tim is telling me to do this.'

'What else did he tell you?'

Madsen's smile was a grimace.

'What did he tell you about the poker?'

Madsen moved his hands about.

'About his pictures?'

The hands fluttered. 'I tell you all I remember . . . I am so tired and in the whirl . . . you know? Perhaps I forget things. . . .'

'Perhaps you do,' Gently said.

'I am still ver' tired. I don' sleep well.'

'You remembered to lose the key,' Gently said.

Madsen just shifted his hands.

Gently puffed. 'You do well,' he said. 'You give a good performance, Madsen. Where are the gloves you're always wearing?'

Madsen opened his eyes. 'I am not wearing gloves.'

'Good,' Gently said. 'So we'll print the poker, the drawer, the picture and the door. Was there anything else you handled, Madsen?'

Madsen swallowed. 'I don' remember . . .'

'If you're lying we'll know it,' Felling said.

'Yes,' Madsen said. 'Yes. You'll know.'

*   *   *

They went down the stairs to the garage, Felling locking the door behind them with care; into the still, closed-up atmosphere of petrol, oil and oily metals. With the lamps switched on there was a half-light. It had a submarine quality. The garage resembled a grimy tank into which at intervals rubbish had been thrown. The two trucks, heavy and cold, lay on the bottom like sunken ships. From a long way above, from the surface, came the chipping of sparrows in a gutter. Gently entered, then Madsen. Madsen was flushed and had his head drooping. Felling came behind jingling his keys. The door creaked slowly over the sunlight.

'Where's your log-book?' Gently asked.

'Yes, in my cab,' Madsen said.

'Fetch it down.'

Madsen hoisted himself up, reached for the book, jumped down. Gently took it, riffled the pages. They were scribbled in pencil in a child-like hand. They gave dates, loadings, places, the names of consigners and consignees.

'Were you legal partners or just associates?'

'Yes, legal partners,' Madsen said. 'I have a deed in my tin box. Legal partners, everything common.'

'But it was Teodowicz who kept the record?'

'Yes, I do not well understand that. Tim was ver' clever, knew all about things. My tax, too: he do that.'

'So now the record has gone up the spout?'

Madsen's head drooped further. 'I'm ver' sorry.'

'You'll be sorrier still when the tax people hear of it.'

'It is wrong, I know. I am sorry.'

Gently riffled some more pages. The scribblings recorded a far-reaching odyssey. Cardiff, Glasgow, Inverness, Yarmouth, Chatham, Bristol, Plymouth. Week after week the Leyland had roamed its vast tally of grey miles, spanning the country as of course, linking margin with margin; occasionally halted by a wheel-change, a snow-blizzard, a broken part, but always rolling again soon, thrusting forth on its appointed way.

'Teodowicz did similar journeys to this?'

'Oh, yes,' Madsen said. 'It is all the same. We do not do the short-haul trips—do not pay so well, you know?'

'Was there any trip he always made—rather than let you make it?'

'Oh, no. It is as it comes. The one who is free takes the load.'

'So you know everything that goes on?'

'There is nothing goes on,' Madsen said.

'There better hadn't be,' Felling said. 'Don't think burning that stuff fools us.'

'I tell you it is honest,' Madsen said. 'I don' have nothing I want to hide. It is ver' foolish what I do, but not to hide nothing. Just being a fool.'

Gently snapped the book shut, handed it to Felling. 'Take care of that for the moment,' he said. He looked at Madsen. 'You're a mechanic?' he asked. 'You do your own servicing here?'

'Oh yes, our own servicing, yes.'

'You know what these tools and materials are used for?'

'Yes, I'm a ver' skilled mechanic.'

'What use do you have for Rangoon oil?'

'Rangoon oil . . .?' Madsen faltered.

'Yes, Rangoon oil,' Gently said. 'There's a half-full bottle on the back of the bench.'

He moved across, reached over the bench, picked out a bottle from a collection of rubbish. It was one of the size of a small medicine bottle and carried a crudely printed, oil-soaked label. The label said: Finest Quality RANGOON OIL* Semmence, Jackson & Co. Ltd. (Mfgs.) Coventry.

'What's this for?' Gently asked.

Madsen's head began to shake. 'I do not know . . . is Tim's, perhaps. I don' know nothing about that.'

'You're a mechanic—and don't know?'

'Yes—perhaps to stop tools from rusting.'

'Tools already covered in grease?'

'That is what I think.' Madsen's flush had left him.

'It's used for tools all right,' Gently said.

'Yes, as I say. Is used for tools.'

'But the tools are guns,' Gently said.

Madsen's hands moved. He didn't speak.

'Well?' Gently said.

Madsen swayed. 'I tell you . . . is something of Tim's,' he said.

'Tim had a gun?'

'I . . . do not know.'

'He was certainly killed with one,' Gently said.

'I do not know about a gun.'

'Nor about this bottle?'

Madsen's head shook.

'Never saw it there—or Tim using it?'

Madsen kept on shaking his head.

46

'You're very unobservant,' Gently said. 'I saw the bottle soon after I came in here.'

'I tell you I know nothing about it,' Madsen said. 'I don' never have a gun. You have searched. There is not one.'

'We haven't dragged the river yet,' Gently said. 'We may get round to it if people keep lying.'

'It is right, I never have one,' Madsen said.

Gently stared at Madsen. Felling sucked in breath.

4

Still in the garage.

Madsen had gone, stumbling over the threshold in his eagerness. Gently stood staring at the greasy bottle. Felling, scowling, eased from foot to foot. They could hear Madsen cross the yard and go up his stairs: the slam of his door. Then only the noises of the sparrows scratching down through the tight air.

Felling said: 'It won't have prints, sir—too much oil on it to take them.'

Gently nodded. He held up the bottle between himself and the light. He unscrewed the cap, sniffed, screwed the cap back on. Felling watched. He kept scowling. There was sweat on both their foreheads.

'So,' Gently said, 'what do you make of it, Felling?'

Felling shifted, inclined his head. 'I think they were running a racket sir, between them. And that's why Madsen burned the papers.'

'You saw something suspicious when you looked at them?'

' . . . No, sir. I can't say that I did. Only I didn't look at them very carefully, I didn't know that it mattered, then.'

'What sort of a racket?' Gently asked.

Felling gave his shoulder a twist. 'Pinching stuff, sir, it could be. Loading a bit more than the docs show, then flogging it off before making delivery.'

Gently said, 'It could have been that.'

'That's one of the rackets,' Felling said. 'Or they might have been knocking off other trucks, sir. There's no saying what they were up to.'

'It could have been that too,' Gently said. 'But where does this mysterious visitor fit into it?'

'Maybe they're two separate things, sir.'

Gently said, 'Yes. Maybe.'

He said: 'Teodowicz' life would seem to have been a busy one, what with running rackets and being an agent. He couldn't have had a lot of time left over. Not for driving loads, things like that.'

Felling grinned. 'I see your point, sir. I was just trying to explain Madsen's behaviour.'

'Yes,' Gently said, 'it interests me too.'

'There could've been something that needed covering up, sir'.

Gently kept on looking at the bottle. His fingers were covered with oil from it. The creases of his face had no expression. He looked at the bottle, turning it slowly.

Felling said: 'I still think that Kasimir bloke is the only answer to the shooting, sir. I don't reckon Teodowicz was a spy or anything, but there's nobody else in the picture.'

Gently held up the bottle. 'Have you an explanation for this?' he asked.

'Oh, I don't know sir,' Felling said. 'Perhaps it belonged to Teodowicz, like Madsen says.'

'Then one or other of them had a gun.'

'It might just have been used for something else, sir.'

Gently's head shook slowly. 'Not what's in this bottle. The Rangoon oil might. But not this stuff.'

Felling hesitated. 'But isn't it Rangoon oil, sir?'

Gently shook his head again. 'You can see. It's bluish. Rangoon oil has a yellow tint—and it doesn't smell of citronella.'

Felling stared at the bottle too.

'Then what do you reckon this stuff is, sir?'

Gently said, 'It's gun-cleaning fluid. From a service source. Perhaps the aerodrome you mentioned.'

The noise of the sparrows; the bottle held up; the trucks brutal in their size. The perfectly still hot air with its lading of petrol and stale oil. The submarine light on the two faces. One expressionless. One puckering.

Felling murmured: 'It's a coincidence, sir. . . .'

'Yes,' Gently said. 'I was thinking the same. What was the name of that aerodrome again?'

'Huxford, sir.'

'Yes, Huxford,' Gently said.

He lowered the bottle, looked about the bench, found a balled-up page of a newspaper. He wiped the bottle on a piece of rag, wrapped the bottle and slipped it into his pocket. He looked at Felling.

'I'll leave the dabs to you,' he said. 'And the check on those cafés, where Teodowicz ate his last meal. And I'd like a couple of men to search this area, all these yards and derelict buildings. Can you manage that?'

'Yes sir,' Felling said. 'Freeman and Rice can do the search.'

'Tell them to keep an eye on Madsen,' Gently said.

'You bet I will, sir. We'll tab that chummie.'

Gently nodded, led the way to the side entry. Felling produced the keys. They went out into the sun.

*   *   *

Four p.m. on the Thursday, and Offingham very nearly asleep. Gently's car shimmered the air over it and opened its door like a broached kiln. He got in, drove down the High Street, across the Market, over the bridge; past two lines of greyed yellow-brick council houses, a couple of pubs, a filling station. Finally a third pub, standing thwartwise at the slovenly road junction, shouldered hard on the beaten passage of the A1 itself.

He halted there to choose his moment, then slid out into

50

the stream. One car, two, went thrusting by him before the Rover picked up its stride. A tall articulated panted ahead of him, dark smoke puffing from its side. It was making fifty and the Rover needed all its guns to overtake. And so on southwards. Under a pale hazed sky.

Everham appeared, a slight congealing of the patchy drab ribbons. A chaffy triangle with a back road, a shop blazing with Dayglo posters. A blind red-brick church flat among dusty dark trees, a phone-box, an indistinct pub, a track worn in the bald verge. And then, for once, the ribbons faltered and gave way completely to grubby hedges; with behind them straw-coloured fields, folding slightly, weighted with hedge-oaks. In the hazy distance, travelling like giants with their feet below the middle horizon, peered the three pink churns of Bintly power station, self-contemplative and aloof.

Another mile. An R.A.C. box. A belt of sloe bushes to the right. To the left, southwards, the changing plane of the shallow roof of a hangar. Then the sign: Lay-By 100 yards, painted freshly black and white; and the ribbed concrete morosity of the lay-by beyond.

Gently slowed, picked a gap, pulled over and parked on the lay-by. It was a small one, designed for no more than two or three vehicles. Because the verge there was narrow the lay-by was pushed back into the hedge; the hedge was thin and had several gaps, and behind it ranged the thicket of sloe bushes. Gently got out. Underfoot the concrete was stained with plentiful oil-marks. Near the south end was a lighter area which had been recently washed off with a broom. Owing to the set-back a small vehicle parked there would be largely concealed from approaching traffic, but an observer stationed there would be able to spot headlights for about half a mile. Wrappers, paper, were strewn on the verge. In the ditch, a rusted bike frame.

He approached the hedge, the gaps in which showed signs

of recent and frequent use. He stepped through it. Behind the hedge lay human faeces and paper. Into the sloe thicket, which was dense, went several tunnels or passages, as though a wild beast had made its lair there in the close gloom of the thorns. One of the tunnels opened opposite to the washed-off concrete. He ducked his head and went into it. Its under-foot soil was compact and unimpressionable. A few feet into the bushes it expanded into a little chamber, and here also lay faeces, paper rubbish, an old saucepan. He turned about and peered through the twigs. He was looking through the gap to the washed-off concrete. Several of the twigs were smashed and singed and hung withered from bleached fibrous stumps. He turned again, went on following the tunnel. From here it had not been used very often. The ground was still hard, but it had grown a little moss, and new twigs projected to obstruct his passage. Some of these new twigs were snapped and withered and some of the moss was slightly compressed. He went on following. He came out of the sloe bushes. Be-yond them was a stubble field, hedges, more fields. Far away southwards, peeking just above low trees, was a roof painted dull red. No other building was in sight.

He returned slowly through the tunnel, examining the walls of it more carefully. The sloe-twigs ended each in a spike and not all the outstanding spikes had been broken. Some yards down the tunnel he paused: a spike low down showed a wisp of snagged wool. It had been caught from a garment moving in a direction away from the road and was of a darkish grey-blue, the colour of certain service uniforms. He felt in his pocket, found an old envelope, stroked the wool off the spike into it. Then he searched for some while longer, but the single wisp was all he found.

Sweating, for it was hot among the sloe bushes, he returned to the lay-by and the car.

* * *

52

'Have you a pass, sir?'

The S.P. from the guardroom was wearing his shirt sleeves rolled and had a white arm-band. Both his arms and his face were sunburned as though he spent his off-duty hours working for a farmer. Gently pulled out his wallet, showed the warrant card. The S.P. looked at him sharply, knowingly.

'Yes sir, I see,' he said, after a slight pause. 'I didn't know sir. We weren't advised in the guardroom.'

'Weren't advised about what?'

'About the civvie police being called, sir. I thought our own blokes were going to handle it.'

Gently shrugged. 'Could be two other people, but I've come here on my own business,' he said. 'I want to talk to your commanding officer. Perhaps you'll ring and let him know.'

'The commanding officer . . . oh, I see, sir!' The S.P. coloured, looked embarrassed. 'Wing-Commander Thompson is on leave, sir, and the acting C.O. is visiting Cardington.'

'Then who do you suggest I should see?'

'The Adjutant, sir. Flight-Lieutenant Withers.'

'Where do I find him?'

'In H.Q., sir. Straight ahead and first right.'

The S.P. stood back a pace and saluted, elbow angled, hand vibrating. Gently grinned a little sombrely, eased in the clutch, let the Rover drift. The wheels bumbled on the concrete roadway, much cracked and much repaired. On either hand, Nissen buildings; ahead the bleached levels of the airfield. He made the right turn. H.Q. was also a Nissen building. On one side of its doors was bolted a notice-board, on the other an out-of-bounds notice. He parked, went in through the doors. Ahead stretched a dim corridor laid with blue linoleum. The linoleum was very highly polished and the smell of the polish hung in the air. On the doors off the corridor were affixed signboards: Central Registry, Pay Accounts, Orderly Room; and at the end of the corridor, Adjutant's Office: F/Lt. Withers (PLEASE KNOCK). Gently knocked and went in. There were two men in the room. One sat at a desk and had shoulder ribbon. One sat at a table. Both looked up.

'Flight-Lieutenant Withers?' Gently asked.

The man at the desk looked annoyed. 'I'm Flight-Lieutenant Withers,' he said. 'And who exactly are you?'

'Superintendent Gently, Central Office.'

'Central Office?' Withers still looked annoyed. 'I didn't know we'd applied to the Central Office,' he said. 'I was under the impression that the affair was domestic.'

'I haven't been applied for,' Gently said.

'Not applied for?'

'Not by you. I'm here entirely under my own steam. To make some inquiries you might help me with.'

'And you're not interested in our little flap?'

'Not', Gently said, 'as far as I know.'

'Well, I'm blowed,' Withers said, easing backwards. He repeated that: 'Well, I'm blowed.' He looked less annoyed. 'You'll have to excuse us,' he said. 'We tend to think in terms only of Huxford. Right at the moment we've got a flap going which is quite absorbing, in its small way.'

'So I gathered,' Gently said.

'Quite absorbing,' Withers said. 'But I doubt whether you'd find it in your class, so we'd better stick to official business. What are these inquiries you've come about?'

'They're to do with sten guns,' Gently said.

'Sten guns. Ah.' Withers looked intelligent. 'Yes indeed. Now I see where we are. Jonesie,' he said to the man at the table, 'run along and rustle up some char, Jonesie.'

'Jonesie can stay,' Gently said.

'Cancel order,' Withers said. 'In fact, we'd better have

54

Jonesie with us. He probably knows more about it than I do. How long have you been at Huxford, Jonesie?'

The man at the table considered this. He was a short man with scanty hair and a solemn face and a turned up chin. He looked some years older than the service limit and had a long grill of red Vs on his tunic sleeve. In a Welsh accent he said:

'About 'forty-two, sir. I came here along with the Admin advance party. Flaming winter it was, too, and not a blind bit of coke.'

'Ah, but there was a war on, Jonesie,' Withers said. 'You couldn't expect luxuries in those days. What were they flying —Maurice Farmans?'

'Cabbage Whites, sir. The Farmans were secret.'

'You're a Welsh liar,' Withers said. 'They were flying Montgolfiers in your day.'

'No, they were grounded, sir,' Jonesie said. 'It was like I told you, we couldn't get the coke.'

'He always caps me,' Withers said. 'I don't know why I put up with Jonesie. The trouble is he runs Huxford, I'd post him tomorrow but the place would collapse. So what do we know about Sten guns, Jonesie?'

Jonesie considered again, then shook his head. 'They were withdrawn in June of 'forty-eight, sir. Don't think we've held any Stens since then.'

'Not even of any kind?'

'No sir. Not official. There'd been a flap about them the year before. Some of the lads had been cutting down pheasants with them and the local gentry got a bit cheesed. So they were withdrawn, sir, by a special A.M.O., and now they go poaching with the Lee Enfields.'

'And the gentry are happy with that?' Withers asked.

'Oh yes sir. I haven't heard any complaints.'

'Keep your ear to the ground, Jonesie,' Withers said. 'I

wouldn't like to hear of them using Bofors.' He turned to Gently. 'The oracle has spoken. We're not holding Sten guns, not even of any kind.'

'Not officially,' Gently said. 'But mightn't there be a few strays about?'

'Over to Jonesie,' Withers said. 'What's the strays situation, Jonesie?'

'I couldn't be precise, sir,' Jonesie said.

'Jonesie,' Withers said, 'be imprecise.'

'Well sir, you know the lads aren't particular when it comes to Air Force property. There's a little quiet flogging goes on, unbeknown to the authorities. And I daresay a Sten will fetch its price if it's taken to the right people. And returns are only figures, you know, which is very abstract information.'

'Yes,' Withers said. 'I'm receiving you, Jonesie.'

'So there may be strays,' Jonesie said. 'And to tell you the blind horrible truth, sir, it would be a miracle if there weren't any.'

'And do you know of any?' Withers asked. 'We want the hard facts here, Jonesie.'

Jonesie looked down his nose. 'I wouldn't like to swear to it on oath, sir. Perhaps the armourers can tell you, they may have some knocking about there. And maybe there were some left in stores. Though you'll be lucky to trace them there.'

'Loud and clear,' Withers said. 'Strength niner, over and out.' He, too, looked down his nose. 'Absorbing,' he said. 'Quite absorbing.' He rose from the desk, a tall, thin man. 'We'd better adjourn to the armoury,' he said.

'Does this connect with your flap?' Gently asked.

'I think its going to collide with it,' Withers said. 'But first things first. We'll try the armoury. Jonesie, you'd better come along too.'

*   *   *

He strode away from the administrative block with long, rangy, stooping steps, Jonesie trotting along by his side, Gently following behind them. Across on the airfield a Proctor aircraft stood with its engine nested in trestles, from a distant dispersal came the tormented bellow of a piston engine being test-run.

'Looks just like life,' Withers said over his shoulder. 'But we were due to close six years ago. Now they've grounded the last Spitfire there's damn all left for us to do.'

'What is your job here?' Gently asked.

'Special maintenance,' Withers said. 'We keep the museum stuff in the air. You want a Wimpey? We've got one.'

He crossed the approach road and inclined left. Jonesie neatly inclined with him. Ahead was an alley of Nissen buildings in which were parked a Hillman van and a box-like truck. The doors of the buildings had identifications painted on them like the doors in H.Q. The buildings housed Radio Mechs, Instrument Reps, Armourers and Electricians.

'The ancillary trades,' Withers said. 'But never mention it in their hearing. The word means a female slave, you know, and there'd be a riot if someone told them.'

He pushed on into the armoury. It consisted of a long, concrete-floored workshop. On the far side, under the windows, ran a wide bench topped with zinc. On the bench lay a couple of Brownings, one of them with its mechanism dismantled; the floor-space was occupied partly by bicycles and partly by stacks of electrically-operated bomb racks. An airman in overalls was mending a puncture at the bench. Two others sat smoking, one on the bench, one on a tool-box. The armoury smelt of thin oil. The smell had a peculiar edge to it.

'Don't get up,' Withers said, whisking straight through the workshop. The three men were staring guiltily and the cigarettes had suddenly vanished. At the end of the workshop two walls of grey slab enclosed a small inner room, by the door of which, mounted on hard-board, was a leave rosta and sheaf of D.R.O.'s. The identification said: Flt. Sergeant Podmore. Withers went in without tapping. A beefy man sitting at a table whisked a duplicated sheet over a football coupon. He got up noisily.

'Ah,' Withers said. 'Flight-Sergeant Podmore, Superintendent. He's the man who'll know most about the subject you're interested in.'

Podmore looked at Gently unhappily, gave the sheet an extra twitch.

'The subject is Sten guns,' Gently said. 'I'd like to know if you keep any here.'

Podmore cleared his throat. 'Sten guns,' he said. 'Don't know about that, sir. We haven't held any since I've been here. There might be an odd one floating around.'

'Have you seen one?'

Podmore hesitated. 'Miller!' he called through the door. The airman who had been mending a puncture came forward, halted, snapped his heels clumsily.

'Dusty,' Podmore said, 'where's that Mark II Sten got to—the one that's always hung around here. See if you can find it up for me.'

'It's in the junk box, Sarge,' Miller said.

'Fetch it here,' Podmore said.

Miller went to a box pushed under the bench, poked around it, took something out. He brought it into the office. It was the frame of a stirrup-pump butted Sten. The barrel and cocking pin were missing and the breech block slid harmlessly in its chamber. Podmore took it, exhibited it to Gently.

'That's the only Sten we've got in the place, sir. Don't ask me when and how it got here—part of the furniture, that's what it is.'

Gently only glanced at it. 'Has it never had a barrel?'

'No sir. Not that I can ever remember.'

58

'Have you heard of any buckshee Stens about the station?'

'No sir. Unless they've got some at stores.'

'Yes,' Withers said. 'Never mind the stores, Sergeant, that's an angle we're coming to in a couple of minutes.'

'Well, you never know what they've got stuck away there, sir,' Podmore said.

'Or alternatively,' Withers said, 'what they haven't. Message received.'

Gently felt in his pocket, brought out the bottle, unwrapped it, stood it on the table.

'Take a look at that, Sergeant,' he said. 'Tell me what it means to you.'

Podmore picked it up, turned it, stared with cautious rounded eyes.

'Just what I think about it, sir?'

'Yes,' Gently said. 'Just what you think about it.'

'Well sir, I'd say the bloke it belonged to had owned a gun for some time. A bottle like this goes a long way, and he'd emptied the bottle at least once. Then he got it filled with this stuff, which you can't buy in the shops, so I'd say he was either a serviceman or had a pal who was one. Probably had a pal, sir. Or he'd have been using gun-cleaning fluid in the first place. And I'd like to know,' Podmore said, 'who's been dishing this out to the civvies.'

'So would I,' Gently said. 'You hold supplies of it, do you?'

'Technical stores do,' Podmore said. 'We only draw it as we need it. But there's plenty here. We'd never miss a little bottle-full like that.' He looked suddenly through the door. 'Dusty,' he said. 'Come here, Dusty.'

Miller had been shrinking out of the doorway. Now he came back, stood looking shamefaced.

'Dusty,' Podmore said. 'You wouldn't know anything about this, would you?'

Miller swallowed. 'I think that's the bottle the W.O. had,' he said.

'Warrant-Officer Sawney?' Podmore said.

'I think its the one,' Miller said. 'He asked me to fill it with fluid for him. Said he'd bought himself a four-ten.'

'Sawney,' Podmore repeated. 'Warrant-Officer Sawney.'

Withers sighed. 'I'm afraid this is where our dirty washing becomes public,' he said.

*   *   *

He dismissed Miller from the office, closed the door and bolted it. He looked wry-faced at Gently. He had a creased face, like a harassed schoolmaster's.

'We've got the peelers in,' he said. 'The service C.I.D. from Headquarters. They're trying to figure out the size of the racket that's been going on in the stores. They're trying to find the stores chiefie too. Somebody squeaked and he took off. They reckon he's flogged off enough stores to set up a brand-new station.'

'Warrant-Officer Sawney?' Gently asked.

'Yes, Sawney,' Withers said. 'A cockney fellow, comes from Chiswick. Only had a couple of years to do. A pal of yours, wasn't he, Jonesie?'

'No pal of mine,' Jonesie said. 'But him and me came here together, we're two of the old originals, like. But don't go calling us pals, sir. It will give the Superintendent the wrong impression.'

'Well, anyway, you knew him,' Withers said. 'He always seemed a bit of a spiv—store-bashers do, as a matter of interest, but there was something especially spivvy about Sawney. He'd got a big nose and a wide grin, you always felt he was trying to have you. And long arms, like a gorilla. Used to be a boxing man at one time.'

'How did you get on to him?' Gently asked.

'Somebody squeaked, as I said. They rang the guardroom last Monday night and told us that Sawney was on the flog.'

'What time was that?'

'Around twelve thirty a.m. We haven't been able to trace the call. The corporal who took it says the voice sounded foreign—you know, very correct, but un-English.' He stopped. He looked hard at Gently. 'That's rather absorbing don't you think?'

'Very absorbing,' Gently said. 'What did the corporal do about it?'

'Nothing just then,' Withers said. 'He thought maybe it was a joke or somebody being malicious. But then, in the morning, he passed it on to me, and I passed it on to the acting C.O. And the C.O. thought he'd better look into it, so he buzzed the stores for Sawney to report to him. And that was where the balloon went up. Sawney wasn't at the stores, wasn't at his billet. We called him on the tannoy, asked people to report on him, but no Sawney. He'd taken a powder.'

'When was he last seen?' Gently asked.

'On the Monday night, in the Sergeants' Mess. He was having his usual beery session, didn't seem to have anything on his mind. But this is what you might call the pay-off—he had a telephone call, too. According to witness it was around twenty-past twelve, and whatever it was it seemed to sober him. He left the mess, drove off in the store's Hillman, and that's positively the last we've seen of him.'

'Have you found the van?'

'Yes,' Withers said. 'It was parked in the yard at Baddesley station. Euston one way, Glasgow the other. They remember several airmen, but they can't pinpoint Sawney.'

'Is his house covered?'

Withers nodded. 'Our police can stumble along pretty effectively. His house has been covered since Tuesday afternoon, and we're reasonably certain he hasn't contacted his wife. But that telephone call . . . the two telephone calls. In my humble opinion, they add together rather neatly. I think he was warned that we were going to be tipped. I don't like to surmise any further than that.'

'Holy St. David,' Jonesie said. 'You don't think it was him who duffed up the Pole, sir?'

'You're being prematurely conclusive,' Withers said. 'You'd better leave that line of thought to the Superintendent.'

'Yes sir, but I've just remembered something,' Jonesie said. 'We used to have Poles here in 'forty-three, sir. Flying Whitleys and Halibashers they were in those days, and throwing them around like old prams. And Sawney was thick with some of those Poles, he used to go around and booze with them. It may not mean a bloody blind thing, sir, but I thought the Superintendent might like to know.'

'Well, fancy,' Withers said. 'You could be right, too, Jonesie.'

'Would you remember any names?' Gently asked.

'Gracious no,' Jonesie said. 'There's no remembering Polish names. It takes a Russian to pronounce them.'

'Nothing like Teodowicz or Kasimir?'

'Nothing half so simple, sir. But you could get on to Records at Ruislip, sir, they'll probably still have the documents.'

'They will indeed,' Withers said. 'This is becoming ultra-absorbing. I think you should talk to our peelers, Superintendent. I feel you're going to have a lot in common.'

'Yes,' Gently said, 'where shall I find them?'

'In the stores, where else,' Withers said. 'I'll take you over to them now. Before they go to tea, or something.'

5

Thursday, five-forty-five p.m. A faint breeze across Huxford airfield. A breeze smelling of sun-dried grass, tansies, one hundred octane and glycol. An arid breeze, spreading the heat collected over the plane geometry of the runways, scarcely lifting the flaps of engine-covers or moving the vane above flying-control. Around the perimeter, cycling figures in oil-stained working-dress uniform, soiled webbing side-packs slung over their shoulders, dope-painted mugs clinking on their lamp-brackets; cycling wearily round the great circumference, all proceeding in one direction; converging into groups and a steady stream past the guardroom, towards the domestic sites. Two N.C.O.s stepping briskly. An officer, keeping his eyes to himself. A clay-daubed Works & Bricks truck with navvies sitting on a plank in the back. The tea-time exodous at Huxford, draining personnel from A to B, leaving here a clerk, there a duty man, whose chits had been honoured by the mess earlier. And in the guardroom four S.P.s. And in the stores, two other men.

*   *   *

The stores was a long, wide Nissen building with khaki-washed plastered ends; having in each end green-painted double doors and at one end a yard enclosed with steel-mesh netting. There were notices pinned to one of the doors announcing a clothing parade and details of boot repairs, signed: A. L. W. Sawney, W.O., i/c Stores, and incorporating a warning about sabotaged garments. The name appeared again painted on the door opposite, and once more, on a board, on the office door inside. The store interior smelled of concrete dust and leather. Apart from the slab-walled office it was open down its length. Facing the door was a wide counter, beyond it tall ranges of metal rack-shelves, against each wall steel lockers, open crates and bins. The smell of leather came from piles of boots which lay strewn on the floor, a ticket tied to each pair.

Withers led in, and into the office. It was a small room cluttered with metal filing-cabinets. At a desk sat a bold-faced man in rank uniform noting details from some forms on to a sheet of paper. Beside him, on his knees at a filing-cabinet drawer, a flight-sergeant was staring at some forms out of a file.

'Squadron-Leader Campling,' Withers said. 'This is Superintendent Gently of Scotland Yard. He's making inquiries about the death of that Pole, and it seems likely that they may coincide with your inquiries.'

Campling looked at both of them without saying anything for a moment. He had brown eyes under thick brows, a straight thick nose, a dimpled chin. 'Oh,' he said. 'Pleased to meet you.' He rose and stuck out his hand. 'I heard you were down here on the Teodowicz case. I didn't think I was going to meet you.'

Gently shrugged. 'Teodowicz was killed with a Sten gun,' he said. 'We naturally want to know where it came from, and Huxford is nearest and handiest.'

'Yes, it is,' Campling said. 'Are you having any luck?'

'Not as yet. But I've a feeling that I'm getting quite warm.'

Campling said: 'Hah,' and exchanged looks with the flight-sergeant. 'I think you're more than warm,' he said. 'I think you're smack on the target. Brennan,' he said to the flight-sergeant, 'show the Superintendent what we found. It did flit through my mind that there might be a connection.'

Brennan got up off his knees. 'Out in the store, sir,' he said. He opened the counter-flap, turned right, went down the aisle next to the outer wall. A bored-looking corporal lounged in the aisle, a cigarette concealed under his hand. He winced slightly and vanished among the rack-shelves, leaving the smell of cigarette-smoke behind him. From across the store came the gulping sound of someone pouring liquid from a Thermos.

'This is it, sir,' Brennan said, stopping at a gap between two lockers. 'You'll notice how the curve of the Nissen wall leaves a space behind these fixtures. There was a dump of obsolete gas-equipment in this gap, stuff that ought to have been returned to Central Stores, and we just happened to move it, out of curiosity, and this is what we spotted behind a locker.'

He pointed to a small, stout wooden case which stood on the floor between the lockers. It was about twenty inches by twelve, had two rope handles, was painted with a green wood preservative. On the lid was roughly stencilled: STEN MK II 6 AM.

'What's inside it?' Gently said.

Brennan reached down, lifted the lid. The lid had originally been nailed into place but it had been prized up and stood loose on the nail points. The case contained five guns, two above, three below; a number of long, narrow magazines; and the space for a sixth gun.

'Any ammunition?' Gently asked.

'Yes sir.'

Brennan opened the door of a locker. He removed a number of empty cartons from the lowest shelf, and finally an unpainted wooden box. In the wooden box were three cardboard boxes and in each cardboard box two fibre cartons. The cartons each contained 250 rounds of 9 mm. rimless (Sten) ammunition. There was a fourth box. This was empty.

'Are these shown on the inventory?' Gently asked.

'Not on any inventory we've found,' Brennan said. 'But they're not alone when it comes to that. About half this stuff isn't on the inventory.'

'What have the stores people got to say about it?'

'They're pleading ignorance.' Brennan made a grimace. 'They're blaming the whole thing on Sawney. But we've hardly got started on them. Yet.'

Gently nodded. 'Take charge of this stuff. Try not to handle it more than you have to.'

'Yes,' Brennan said. 'Don't worry about that, sir. I've done some training down at Ryton.'

Gently returned to the office. Campling sat toying with a retractable ball pen.

'Well?' he said, snapping the pen. 'Is it homicide as from now?'

Gently shrugged, looked round for a seat, settled for a tool-box stood on end. Withers was squatting on another box and puffing evenly at a Lovat-pattern briar.

'Tell me about this business,' Gently said. 'What's the extent of it? How long has it gone on? What were the channels Sawney was using? Who do you think was in it with him?'

Campling grinned, snapped the pen. 'Easy questions, difficult answers. We haven't got to the bottom of this thing yet, but I'll give you a run-down as far as we've gone. The racket was a pretty steady racket. It'd been going on for at least two years. During that time . . . these are very rough figures . . . I'd say that Sawney netted around fifteen thousand pounds. It may have been a good deal less than that, it depends on what he got for the stuff. And it wouldn't all be going into his pocket. There had to be someone else in the deal.'

'How did he work it?'

Campling clicked his tongue. 'By the oldest and hoariest dodge we know of. Really, it makes you blush with shame, just going through these old indent forms. Take a look at one.'

He picked a form off the desk and handed it to Gently. It was printed to facilitate the ordering of stores and to ensure that a fixed procedure was complied with. Beneath a detailed identification was a ruled-off compartment for the insertion of the items, and beneath this spaces for signatures and stamps without which the order would not be authorized. The form had been made out. Station, unit, section were entered. A list of items filled the first ten lines of the compartment. Under these was drawn a line and two other lines, to close the compartment; stamps, signatures were in place, and a cancelling stamp from Central Stores.

'Impressive, isn't it?' Campling said. 'Can you spot where he worked the fast one?'

'Hmn,' Gently said. 'This last item looks a little bit screwed up.'

'You see?' Campling said. 'You're not a fraud man, but even you can spot that. Yet for two solid years that fellow's been getting away with the trick. Instead of drawing his line on the rule he's drawn it in the space underneath, leaving enough room for an extra entry after the form had been authorized. In this case, five portable charging-sets, worth about a hundred and fifty quid. And these indents were going in every day. No wonder the defence estimates are up.'

'And all tax-free,' Withers said. 'That's the truly criminal part. You can't admire his ingenuity while he's dodging his responsibilities.'

Gently returned the form. 'Has he been specializing in anything?' he asked.

'No,' Campling said. 'He'd got catholic tastes. All was grist that came to Sawney's mill. Tyres, clothes, technical stores, flying-suits, instruments, the lot. It went into the street markets as like as not. We're trying to get a line on that.'

'What are your ideas about the stores staff.'

'The store-bashers?' Campling snapped the ball pen.

'There's a corporal, a couple of store-keepers, two G.D.s and occasional janker-wallahs. The janker-wallahs are purely casual, and the G.D.s rarely stay on one job. I haven't made up my mind about the other three, but my feeling is that they're outside it. We've checked a little. We haven't found any signs of them living above their income. Of course, they knew something was going on, with the stuff that passed through here, but I doubt if they had their fingers in it. Sawney would know how to keep them sweet.'

'So,' Gently said, 'the goods were ordered. The order was dispatched from Central Stores. How did it arrive here?'

'By rail,' Campling said. 'To Baddesley station. Then on to here by the camp transport.'

'And where were they unloaded?'

'In the stores yard behind here—with Sawney doing the checking, of course.'

'And after that?'

Campling snapped the ball pen. 'Perhaps you've got some ideas about that,' he said. 'I don't mind telling you that we've drawn a blank. He couldn't have been using a service vehicle.'

'You're sure of that?'

'Pretty sure,' Campling said. 'Unless half the camp's involved in the racket. The transport section is at the back of the guardroom, everything is checked in and out.'

'What about the vans belonging to the sections?'

'They're parked in a compound on the domestic site. It's at the back of the messes, where they have a night staff, and nobody will admit noticing anything suspicious. But I don't go much on the van idea—the stores van is only five hundred-weight, you know.'

'Would a vehicle coming in have to pass the guardroom?'

'Yes,' Campling said.

'No,' Withers contradicted.

They looked at him.

'I hate to have to admit it,' he said, 'but this airfield is as open as Hampstead Heath. Ask any of the drivers. There's a back way in. It's across on the other side of the drome. There's an old dispersal pan, back in some trees, and you simply drive off it on to a by-road.'

Campling looked bitter. 'Don't you have dispersal guards?'

'As promulgated,' Withers said, 'on S.R.O.s. That is, a couple of sleepy erks patrolling a four-mile perimeter, dotted with comfy kites to doss in, and the duty officer minding his own business. Oh yes, we have our dispersal guard.'

'Where does the by-road lead to?' Gently asked.

'To a farm in one direction,' Withers said. 'And to the A1 in the other.'

'Handy,' Campling said crisply.

'I believe the drivers find it so,' Withers said.

Campling snapped the ball pen twice. Withers puffed, glanced at his wrist-watch.

Gently said: 'Getting back to the site here—who is on duty here at nights?'

'It depends on whether there's night-flying,' Withers said. 'But we don't see much of that these days. There'll be flying-control up in the tower, and the duty orderly room clerk, and the duty driver, and the S.P.s, and the duty electrician in the charging-room. That's the lot.'

'Anyone near the stores?'

'Nobody nearer than the charging-room.'

'Do the S.P.s do any roaming about?'

'Not unless they're called out to something.'

'So it's pretty quiet here in the small hours?'

'Very quiet,' Withers said.

'You could bring a truck in by the back way, and spend an hour loading it up?'

Withers nodded. 'You could do that. If you knew a man. Who had a truck.'

'Yes,' Gently said. 'A man with a truck. But who, one day, might quarrel with you.'

*   *   *

Campling finally dropped the ball pen. He took a cigarette-case out of his pocket. He opened the case, took a cigarette himself, threw one to Brennan, who stood in the doorway. Gently had meanwhile brought out his sand-blast, and now all four men were smoking. The bicycles and footsteps outside had ceased. A motor horn sounded far away, near the gates.

Campling said to his cigarette: 'It's a case. I don't think Sawney's going to be court-martialled. If you want those boxes and cartons dusted, we can do it. Brennan's got his equipment in the guardroom.'

'Have you got Sawney's dabs?' Gently asked.

'Naturally. We took a set off his shaving mirror. And I've got his photograph and full description and all the particulars you'll want.'

'I'd like the stuff printed,' Gently said.

Campling nodded to Brennan. Brennan left. Campling drew in heavily on the cigarette, let the smoke trickle out of his nostrils.

'The bloody fool,' he said. 'Why did he have to do a thing like that? We'd got him for certain on the flogging charge, but that's a technicality in the services.'

'You don't know Sawney,' Withers said. 'Sawney was the type to blow his top.'

'But with a Sten gun?' Campling said. 'Hell and all, man, he must have been bonkers.'

'He was the type,' Withers said. 'Sawney had a nasty bit of a temper. I can imagine him getting the tip-off he was going to be shopped and then taking off with that gun. It's just too bad he had access to one. He could have clobbered the Pole with his bare fists.'

'He must have been insane,' Campling said. 'It was savage what he did. He'll have to plead insanity.'

'Are any murderers sane?' Withers asked, puffing.

'This one isn't,' Campling said. 'I'll stake my discharge on it.' He looked at Gently. 'What are your views?' he said. 'Or is it against protocol for me to inquire?'

Gently stared at the smoke from his pipe. 'I haven't got any views,' he said. 'I'm simply fact-finding.'

Campling laughed. 'If you want it that way,' he said. 'Perhaps the whole discussion is *sub judice* and incompetent. But it's a clear case, I'm afraid. Sawney is for the high jump. And I'm sorry for it. I got the impression he was more of a knave than a criminal.'

'Thank you,' Gently said. 'The reaction of the man on the job is also a fact. And I'm puzzled, that's another fact.' He puffed once or twice. 'Because there's another case against another man which another investigator finds logical. And there seems no connection between the two. Except the shooting of Teodowicz.'

Both of them stared at him.

'This is getting too devious for me,' Campling said. 'What do you want us to do?'

'Just carry on,' Gently said. 'You're better placed than we are to handle this end of the business. Go on clarifying the picture of Sawney's racket and its connections. We'll put out an all-stations for him, and give you a hand tracing his outlets.'

'You mean you're not convinced that Sawney's the man?'

'I'm not convinced or unconvinced.'

Campling shook his head. 'You're a queer lot, up at the Yard,' he said. 'I'd go to court with half this case. But you know your own business best. We'll do what you say, of course. We'd continue to clear up this mess in any case.'

'Have you those particulars for me?'

71

Campling stared at him for a second. Then he reached up a brief-case, opened it, took out some documents.

'These are from Records and consequently sacred.'

'I'll see they're returned in due course.'

'Do,' Campling said. 'Or they'll serve up my head on crossed prop blades.'

The first document was an identity card. It bore a photograph of Sawney. It showed a large-faced man with a slightly-squashed nose and a wide-lipped mouth and small eyes. The eyes were not looking straight at the camera and appeared glazed and absent. The mouth was tilted between a grin and a smile. The flesh under the eyes was puffy. Beneath the photograph was a printed form with typed-out details. Date of Birth: 15.3.19. Height: 6 ft. 0½ ins. Weight: 13 st. 10 lbs. Colouring: brown hair, blue eyes. Scars: 2″ scar, left knee. Distinguishing Marks: broken nose. Married or Single: married. The card was headed, Full Name: Sawney, Albert Leonard Wilfred. Subsequent forms recorded that he was born at Fulham, had an elementary education, entered the service as an apprentice in 1934, was a service heavyweight boxing champion in 1940, 1941, rose progressively to the rank of Warrant Officer (Stores), had been stationed at Tern Hill, Leuchars, Hornchurch, Compton Bassett, Padgate, Matlaske and Huxford, was married in 1947, was presently in receipt of allowances for three children, had been punished for several petty offences including A.W.O.L. and being drunk and disorderly, and was regarded by a succession of commanding officers as Efficient, Conscientious, Skilled in his Trade, Unstable but Conscientious, Conscientious, Conscientious and Efficient, and Conscientious. He had been on several ground defence courses. He was graded as a marksman.

'Ground defence?' Gently queried.

'But of course,' Withers said. 'As though you hadn't enough against him anyway, he's an expert at handling weapons. Rifle, revolver, automatic weapons, and a dab hand with a grenade. I know. I'm a shooting man myself. He was a regular at the range.'

'What else does ground defence consist of?'

'Oh, gas lectures. Field tactics. Crawling for miles on one's stomach. Anything strenuous and unpleasant.'

'And he was good at these things?'

'Yes. He was that sort of bloke.'

'Handy,' Campling said. 'Very handy. And now he's on the run with a Sten.'

Gently nodded at nothing. 'You had Poles stationed here,' he said. 'We don't think Teodowicz was in England during the war, but it's an angle we can't overlook. Could you have the record checked—for a Timoshenko Teodowicz?'

'I'll get on the blower.' Campling made a note.

'Also for a Jan Kasimir. Spelt with a K.' He felt in his pocket. 'Then there's this.' He took out the envelope with its wisp of wool. He went to the desk, shook the wool on to a sheet of paper, put the sheet in front of Campling. 'What would you say it was?'

Campling poked at the wisp. 'It's been snagged off an Air Force uniform,' he said. He was silent a moment. 'That's important,' he said, 'isn't it? It's something that's going to hang Sawney.'

'It's a piece of evidence,' Gently said. 'I want its identification made steam-proof.'

'We can do that for you,' Campling said. He sighed. 'The bloody fool,' he said.

'Now I'd like to talk to that Corporal out there.'

'The bloody fool,' Campling repeated.

*   *   *

The Corporal came in. He was a thin, pale-faced man. He had nicotine-stained fingers. His hands trembled all the time. He was about thirty-five years old. His name was Corporal

Timmins. He had to stand up because there was no seating.

'This is Superintendent Gently of the Yard, Corporal,' Campling told him. 'He wants to ask you some questions.'

Timmins flashed a nervous look at Gently, dropped his eyes, mumbled, 'Yessir.'

'You can stand easy,' Gently said.

Timmins tried to stand easy. His feet dragged apart a little, his hands crept round behind him.

Gently said: 'How long have you been stationed at Huxford, Corporal?'

'About . . . a couple of years, sir,' Timmins mumbled. 'I come here in March 'fifty-nine.'

'Were you a corporal then?'

'Yessir, I was. I was made up a corporal when I come here.'

'You like store work?'

'Yessir, don't mind it. I worked in a warehouse before I come in.'

'How did you get on with Warrant Officer Sawney?'

'Oh, all right sir. He was all right.'

'Pals, were you?'

'Well . . . I don't know, sir.' Timmins stiffened his arms, relaxed them again. 'I wouldn't say we was pals, not like that. He'd got his Tate and Lyle, sir. But he was all right, he was one of the lads. You used to know where you was with him. He took us on the booze now and then.'

'Where did he take you on the booze?'

'Oh, Baddesley, sir . . . Offingham, sometimes. Once we had a do in Bedford, but we didn't go there much.'

'Did he have any friends at these places?'

'Not like friends I don't think, sir. He knew the blokes behind the bar and that sort of thing.'

'Did he talk to the civilians?'

'Well, he passed the time, sir. Like what the Spurs would do to Leicester, and such like. He liked to talk.'

'Did he talk to the transport drivers?'

'Could've done, sir. I can't say.'

'Did he use to go to the Blue Bowl Café in Offingham?'

'Yessir, we'd go in there for a snack.'

'You often went there?'

'Well, now and then, sir. When we wanted something to soak up the beer.'

'Would you say he went there habitually?'

'I wouldn't know about that, sir. We went there with him . . . well, maybe half-a-dozen times.'

'Did he know the waitresses in there?'

'He knew one of them by her name, like.'

'Did he talk to any civilians in there?'

'He may have done sir. I just can't remember.'

'Did he talk to any foreigners?'

'Not that I know of, sir, he didn't.'

'Did he use to go to The Raven roadhouse?'

Timmins relaxed his arms, which had been steadily stiffening.

'Yessir,' he said. 'He used to go there, but he didn't take us along with him.'

'Why was that?'

'Well, sir.' Timmins tried to grin. 'There's a bint in there, it was like that.'

'A woman?'

'Yessir. Wanda, her name is. He was a regular one in there.'

'He used to spend nights with her?'

'I reckon so, sir. Leastways, he was up there a lot of evenings. Let on she was a tidy bit of stuff, and that sort of thing.'

'How often did he go there?'

'Pretty often, sir. Twice a week, I shouldn't wonder.'

'Do you know who he used to meet there?'

'No sir, I was never there with him.'

'Have you been there yourself?'

'A couple of times, sir. Just for a cup of char, that's all.'

'Who did you see there?'

'Well . . . mostly drivers. . . .'

'Anyone you knew?'

'No sir. Nobody at all.'

Gently nodded very slowly, struck a match for his pipe. Timmins strained his arms once or twice, ventured a look towards Gently. Withers sat sideways away from them, nursing his knees and sucking. Campling kept staring at the desk where the wisp of wool lay on the paper. The stores, the sites around them were silent. The office was hot and full of smoke.

Gently said: 'I'm not going to ask you how much you know about what was going on here. I'll put it this way. Could you give me a guess who was in this business with Sawney?'

'None of us wasn't in it, sir,' Timmins mumbled. 'We never had no part in it.'

'You had eyes,' Gently said. 'I'm not asking you to incriminate yourself.'

'No sir,' Timmins said. He pulled on his arms another time. 'It was someone outside, sir,' he said. 'You're right if that's what you're thinking.'

'Who?'

'Don't know, sir.'

'Have you seen him?'

'Not proper I haven't,' Timmins said. 'But he's got a truck, I know that. It wasn't one of our jobs.'

'Tell me about it,' Gently said.

'It was once when I was on guard,' Timmins said. He stopped. He looked half-way towards Withers.

'Oh, carry on,' Withers said. 'I shan't be listening to this bit, Timmins.'

'Yessir,' Timmins said. 'When I was on guard, sir. We use the dispersal hut by number three hangar. There wasn't no night-flying or anything, everybody had packed up. So I thought I might as well drop round to the mess—there's a Wraf I know who works there, sir. So I borrowed one of the erks' bikes—'

'What time would that be?' Gently asked.

'Be about one,' Timmins said. 'I hung on in case the duty officer showed up.'

'Wasn't me,' Withers said to his pipe.

'No sir,' Timmins said. 'I don't remember who it was, sir.'

'I should keep it like that,' Withers said, 'were I you.'

'Yessir,' Timmins said. 'I don't remember. But when I got down here there was a light in the store—not all of them on, just one, I reckon—and there was a truck standing out in the yard, and a couple of blokes were loading stuff into it.'

'And you were on guard?' Campling inquired sourly.

'I did go and look, sir,' Timmins said. 'I wasn't to know it wasn't something proper, we have had calls for stuff during the night.'

'So what else did you see?' Gently said.

'I saw that one of the men was the W.O., sir. And I reckoned it must have been on the up-and-up, though it did strike me as a bit queer at the time.'

'What about the other man?'

'I didn't recognize him, sir. There was only the light coming through the door. But he was a big bloke, like the W.O., and he'd got on one of those khaki jackets.'

'Did you see the truck clearly?'

'It was one of those big jobs, painted a dark colour. Not one of ours.'

'Did you notice the make?'

'I reckon it might have been a Leyland, sir. I didn't pay a lot of attention to that.'

'A Leyland,' Gently said. 'Could the dark colour have been green?'

'Yessir, could have been,' Timmins said.

'Thank you,' Gently said. 'That'll be all for now, Corporal.'

Timmins dragged his feet together, threw up an uncertain salute.

'Hook it,' Campling said tersely. 'I might forget you've been given immunity.'

Timmins slunk to the door, but there halted, partly turning again.

'What's worrying you, Timmins?' Withers asked.

'I was wondering,' Timmins mumbled, 'if we could go to tea, sir?'

Withers chuckled. 'Go on. Clear off. But don't show your nose out of camp.'

'No sir,' Timmins said. 'Thank you, sir.' He went through the door, closing it meticulously.

Campling lit a fresh cigarette, blew fierce smoke at the ceiling. 'Can we tie Sawney in any tighter?' he asked. 'Or won't a simple hanging do for you?'

Gently gave a little shrug. 'It's pretty tight,' he admitted.

'Teodowicz' truck was a Leyland, painted green?'

'Yes,' Gently said. 'But there are two Leylands. Two Leylands, two big men, and possibly two khaki jackets.' He struck another light for his pipe. 'Will Jonesie have gone to tea?' he asked Withers.

'Not till I get back,' Withers said.

'Get him on the phone,' Gently said.

Withers rose from his tool-box, went over to the desk, phoned the Orderly Room.

'What do you want to know?' he asked.

'More about past personnel,' Gently said. 'I seem to remember airmen with Norwegian flags on their shoulders. I'd like you to ask Jonesie if he remembers any being here.'

'Roger,' Withers said. He put the question to the phone.

'Yes,' he said, after a pause. 'Oddly enough, there were some here.'

'Does he remember any names?'

Withers asked. 'No, no names. Apparently there were only one or two, and they were soon remustered somewhere else.'

'Can you get me their names?' Gently asked Campling.

'I'll try,' Campling said. 'Is it important?'

Gently also blew smoke at the ceiling. 'It's an angle,' he said. 'It had better be covered.'

CHAPTER

6

Thursday, in the evening. The August twilight beginning.
The sun melted away indefinitely into a haze of red, orange
and umber. The bleached sky becoming dusty. A single large
and very yellow star. The air thick and sodden with heat and
with the humidity that would be a dew. Beetles flying. A bat
disporting itself like a butterfly, in a quiet corner. A flush of
young starlings going to roost. A partridge scolding from the
stubble. Aircraft, black, swathed, huge, standing silent around
the deserted perimeter, breathing, to a little distance, oil and
glycol and a certain sourness. Number three hangar, closed,
but with a draped Magister standing outside it. A Nissen hut
with bikes stood about it, a couple of starting trolleys, some
gantries, covers. An airman in shirtsleeves appearing at the
door, watching incuriously, vanishing again.

And on the Road the vehicles had sidelights for the light
which was neither one thing nor the other, bating no speed
although the drivers were squinting and reacting less surely
to their problems in velocity. Two had died in the past ten
minutes, having failed in some calculation of differential.
Other mathematics allowed for further mortality at a predict-
able rate per minute. Some of these condemned had read of
Teodowicz. They had been deaf to more distant bells. And
they would die with little stir, though perhaps more fearfully
and no less bloodily. But nobody would hang because of that.
Their deaths were too numerous and commonplace. A
vehicle is a clumsy blunt instrument which can scarcely be
wielded more than once. A small fine, a brief imprisonment,
that would be society's limit. Death itself is unimportant.
Only the weapon has significance.

And the stars began to define themselves above the statistics of the Road, dusting the greyish dim hemisphere with a thousand million of computations, clarifying the terrestial egotism with an index of mild infinity, but unseen: infinitesimally, North and South went its way.

★ ★ ★

Gently came to The Raven.

It was a one-storey timber building and was shaped like an L, with the gable-end of the short stroke nearest to the road. It stood alone. It was two miles from Everham, a mile and a half from Huxford village. Behind the building lay a garden with some fruit trees, but beyond that the fields, and the fields were dark. The interior of the L formed a vehicle park. At the front of the park were three derelict petrol pumps. Near the pumps stood a post carrying a rusted sign. The sign represented an heraldic raven and bore the name beneath in Gothic letters. At the foot of the post was a painted board which read: Transport Café; Meals; Bed and Breakfast. The windows of the short stroke were dimly lighted. The windows of the long stroke were not. A door, set in the short stroke near the angle, had a naked bulb over it and a sign: Open. In the park were two trucks, an articulated, a removal van, a black Mini-Minor and a moped. From the building came the distorted sound of a juke-box playing.

Gently slid the 105 into the park, locked it, stood for some seconds looking at the vehicles. Then he went in. He entered a long room with a service counter opposite the door. Behind the counter stood a woman, and on the counter leaned an airman, talking to her. They both stopped talking to look at him. He went up to the counter.

'Yes?' she said, her face a blank.

'A cup of tea,' Gently said. 'What are you serving?'

'Well, I can do you egg-and-chips. Or a pie. Or some cold meat and salad.'

'Egg-and-chips,' Gently said.

'Bread-and-butter?'

'No, just egg-and-chips.'

She hadn't taken her eyes off him, and now, suddenly, the eyes smiled. Not the mouth, which was small and tight, but the eyes: they unexpectedly flowered.

'You'd like your tea now, I suppose.'

'Yes,' he said. 'I'll have it to go on with.'

She felt under the counter for cup, saucer and spoon without letting her eyes wander away. The airman, a sergeant, looked down into the glass which rested half-empty in his hand. The juke-box hammered to a stop, gritted, clicked and was not re-started. She poured the tea, pushed a sugar-bowl towards him.

'You haven't been here before, have you?' she asked.

Still the eyes and not the face. The face was flattish but with a delicate chin.

'No,' he said. 'This is my first visit.'

'I just thought your face seemed familiar,' she said. 'I'll bring your egg-and-chips if you'll sit down. It shouldn't take five minutes.'

He sat down. He felt hot. He sipped the tea, looked at the room. It held about twenty small square tables, each with four chairs to it. The walls were lined with plaster-board which had been at some time distempered cream and on them were hung a few cockled advertisement cards featuring soft drinks and potato crisps. There were seven other customers, crews of the vehicles parked outside. Four of them sat at one table, eating and talking, one was reading a paper, one had his feet up, snoring. The other one had been playing the juke-box, but now sat solemnly drinking tea. The one with the paper sat at the end of the room and wore a ring that flashed when he turned a page. The room smelt of fried chips, coffee, tobacco-smoke. It was lit by two bulbs and there was one behind the counter.

He kept sipping the tea. The woman had gone through a curtained doorway. From behind it came the hiss of an egg broken into hot fat. The four drivers together were talking about breakdowns which always occurred on a Saturday or a Sunday. The sergeant, a young man with a flushed complexion, reamined leaning on the counter and paying attention to nobody. Beyond where the egg was cooking a door opened and closed: softly. Then somebody attended to the egg.

She brought out his order on a tin tray and set it briskly on the table. She was wearing a sleeveless black dress and beneath it her small breasts rolled nakedly.

'Some sauce?' she asked him.

'Just pepper and salt.'

'You'd better let me fill your cup up.'

Her voice was neutral-toned, fastidious, with a slight contralto huskiness. Several of the men had an eye on her, including the one who was reading a paper. He lowered the paper at the sound of her voice, stared furtively, raised it again. She wasn't pretty. She had a slight figure. She wasn't young. Her expression was unpromising. But her eyes smiled, sometimes. From the whole depth of her body.

'You're sure you wouldn't like some bread-and-butter?'

She hesitated by the table, stooping towards him. The sergeant suddenly put his glass down hard, straightened himself, made a dab at his tie. She looked at him indifferently.

'Oh—are you going now, Johnny?'

He picked up his hat and pulled it on before replying: 'I reckon I am.'

She shrugged slim shoulders. 'You weren't here for very long!'

'No,' he said. His mouth was petulant. 'Think I'll be on my way,' he said.

'You can stay if you like.'

'Yes,' he said. 'Think I'll be on my way.'

'Just as you like.'

He made a business with his tie. 'Goodnight, Wanda,' he said.

'Goodnight, Johnny.'

He finished with the tie, walked out smartly, looking at nobody. A moment later came the racket of the moped and the sound of it being fiercely accelerated.

'He's jealous of you,' Wanda muttered, but without looking at Gently. 'He's a damned little fool, as he'll find out. *I* didn't ask him to come up here.'

'Why should he be jealous of me?'

She shrugged again. 'They get ideas, these kids. They all think you're going to sleep with them. What about that bread-and-butter?'

'No thank you,' he said.

Her eyes found him, smiled. 'You don't have to worry about your figure.'

'I'm not that hungry,' he said. 'It's warm.'

'Well, don't be backward in asking for anything.'

She took the tray, retired to the counter, began to wash and dry saucers and cups. The drivers who sat together, and who had fallen silent, now resumed their conversation. The man beside the juke-box came for another cup of tea. The snorer woke up, stared, went back to sleep. The man with the ring tilted his newspaper to get a good look at Gently eating. He was sitting at the far end of the room and was wearing what appeared to be brand-new dungarees.

'That's a fresh egg,' Wanda said. Gently's table was nearest to the counter. 'I get them from a man up at Everham. Are you certain I haven't seen you before?'

Gently grunted, drank some tea.

'You're not a film star,' Wanda said. 'I shall probably place you, if I think hard. *You're* not in a hurry to go, are you?'

'No,' Gently said. 'My time's my own.'

'I'm glad,' Wanda said. 'I like company. I never keep open later than eleven. Sometimes, if it's slow, I close earlier. I shall probably close early tonight. You're the type who smokes a pipe, aren't you?'

Gently nodded. 'I smoke a pipe.'

'Yes,' Wanda said. 'A real pipe-smoker. A man should always smoke a pipe.'

*　　　*　　　*

Gently smoked his pipe. The trucks, the articulated, left. Eventually the man by the juke-box, a neckless cockney, looked at a pocket-watch and woke the sleeper.

'Time to roll, Alf. We got to see a man.'

The sleeper came to himself with a start. He stared at Gently, blinked his eyes, picked up his cap and took from it a tab end. He lighted the tab end and coughed.

'I been asleep, Len,' he said.

'Blinking telling me,' Len said. 'Like a flipping diesel you sounded.'

'Snoring was I?' Alf asked.

'That's being polite,' Len said. 'Never met a bloke like you. But on your feet chum. We got to roll.'

Alf rose, yawned, stretched, coughed again, drank some dregs from a cup. Wanda, who'd been behind the curtain, ducked through it again. She'd a comb in her hand.

'With you' Alf said. 'Bye, Wanda. Might be through here again Tuesday.'

'Don't do anything I wouldn't,' Wanda said.

'Do us a favour,' Alf said. 'Bye for now.'

'He's got his old woman back,' Len said. 'You don't have to worry about him, Wanda.'

'Bye,' Wanda said.

'Bye,' Len said.

They went out. Len slammed the door.

'Regulars,' Wanda said, coming out from the counter, putting the comb through her hair. A scent of sandalwood came with her. She had touched up her lips with pale red lipstick. 'We used to be a smart place here, you know, until the war put an end to it. My husband ran it. We're divorced. He divorced me. The place has gone down. Is that 105 yours?'

'Yes,' Gently said.

Outside the furniture van was moving out of the park.

'They're a nice car,' Wanda said. 'Not showy, just nice.'

She leaned at the table, looking down at him. She had powdered her face very slightly. She touched her lips with the tip of her tongue and her eyes smiled. She rocked a little towards him. The man with the newspaper rustled the newspaper. Wanda looked sulky, looked towards him.

'Is there anything I can get you?' she asked him.

He fumbled the newspaper nervously.

'I'm just closing,' Wanda said. 'If you want anything you'd better ask for it.'

'No,' he said. 'Nothing I want.' He got the newspaper together. Besides the dungarees he wore a khaki shirt and a slouch cap which also seemed new. He rose from the table. He didn't look towards them. He made for the door. When it closed Wanda went quickly across to it and shot the bolts at the top and bottom. She came back shrugging, laid a hand on Gently's shoulder. The hand laid still, very light.

'Is he a regular?' Gently asked.

'Him? I've never seen him before.'

'Can I use your phone?'

'Of course you can. It's through here, in the parlour.'

She led him behind the curtain and into a small kitchen, switching off the lights in the café as she went. From the kitchen a door led left into a larger room which was dimly lit by a low-wattage lamp. The room was carpeted and furnished with a studio couch and three fire-side chairs; two tables, a larger and a smaller, a pouffe, a book-case, an old radiogram. The furniture was not new but it had been of good quality. On the wall hung a photographed nude. The subject of the photograph was Wanda. The telephone stood on the smaller table.

'There you are. Help yourself. It's a local call, isn't it?'

'Yes,' Gently said. 'Offingham Police Station.'

'Oh, that's all right, that's local.'

She leaned her elbows on the table and watched him hook off the number. Her breasts were compressed between her arms and hung enlarged and defined. He was connected to the desk.

'Gently speaking,' he said. 'I want you to trace the owner of a black Mini-Minor, registration number XOL 7397. Yes. Probably from the town. Yes. Everham 86. Otherwise when I come in. Thank you, sergeant.' He hung up.

'Is that man wanted for something?' Wanda asked.

Gently stared at her, shrugged.

'Well,' she said. 'It's no business of mine. And I'm not in a mood for business, anyway. And now you've told me who you are, but don't think that makes any difference. If I didn't like you you wouldn't be in here. I'm not trying to bribe you with my body.'

'You knew who I was,' Gently said.

Wanda nodded. 'Of course I did. And if you want to ask me a lot of questions go ahead, that's all right by me. But when you've done your job. . . .' Her eyes swam at him. 'Life isn't so very long,' she said. 'You can waste so much time with the proprieties. And opportunity. That's what counts.'

Gently puffed. 'You're a surprising woman.'

'Because I say what I mean?' she asked. 'But don't forget

that I'm a divorcee, I've had all the silliness knocked out of me. It was the co-respondent who took that photograph. It was produced in the court.'

'How long ago?'

'Oh . . . fifteen years. I was thirty-six last March.'

'Where's your husband?'

'He's dead. He was killed in an accident soon after.'

'Hmn,' Gently said. 'Shall I get a warrant, or will you let me search this place?'

'Don't be a bloody fool,' she said. 'Come and search. I'll show you round.'

She led him back through the kitchen and into a corridor beyond. She threw open a door on the left and switched on a light in a bare-looking sitting room.

'That was the residents' lounge—when we aspired to having residents. Now I just get a few bed-and-breakfasts, and they mostly spend their time in the café. I flogged the furniture after the war.'

'Does it pay, this place?'

'I hope I don't look like a millionairess. I break about even after drawing a salary.'

'Who was that bloke in the dungarees?'

'You'd better ask him. He's new here.'

She passed on to an entry. Beyond it were two bathrooms and two toilets. There was also an outer door leading into a concreted yard. On one side of the yard was a fuel shed about one quarter full of small coke, on the other a scullery containing a washing machine, spin dryer, some domestic lumber. Outside the yard, dimly illuminated by a torch Gently shone at it, lay a neglected kitchen garden and some stunted, unpruned fruit-trees. He stood listening. He heard a moan of traffic, an owl hooting in the distant fields.

'You're about half a mile from the lay-by here. Are you sure you didn't hear that shooting?'

From behind him she said: 'If I did, I didn't notice it.'

'How was that?'

'You hear so much of it. There's Huxford just over there. They often fire a burst when they're night-flying. You get so you don't pay it any attention.'

'But this was closer, in a different direction.'

'It wouldn't register, indoors,' she said. 'And the wind has a lot to do with it, too—sometimes it sounds just over the road.'

'Was anyone staying here that night?'

'No.'

'Isn't there a path from here to the lay-by?'

She paused. 'You can get through the fields, but there isn't what you'd call a path. There's a gap in the hedge here. I sometimes walk in the fields.'

'And nobody came that way that night?'

'No.'

'An airman?'

'No. Not an airman.'

'Nobody left a vehicle standing in your park?'

'Not after I closed. As far as I know.'

'How long had that bloke in the dungarees been here?'

'Most of the evening. And I repeat, I don't know him.'

'Let's go back in.'

They walked side by side, she letting him go through the door first. She closed the door and bolted that also, ran a hand lightly over her dew-wet hair.

'The rest is all bedrooms.'

She nodded towards the corridor, which past the entry turned right; traversing the front of the long stroke of the building with a number of doors opening off it to the left. The doors were numbered one to twelve. Gently opened the first of them. Behind it was a room about ten by ten containing a bed, a wardrobe, a dressing-table, two chairs. The wardrobe contained two coat-hangers. The bed was made up but looked flat and unused. The window was ajar but the room smelt stuffy and there was a bloom of dust on the worn buff linoleum.

'When did you last have a bed-and-breakfast?'

'Oh.' She thought about it. 'Last Tuesday week. There was a driver from Newcastle came in with a puncture and stayed the night. You can see my book.'

'Which room did he stay in?'

'He stayed in this room. I only keep a couple of beds made up.'

'Did Tim Teodowicz ever stay here?'

'Of course not—why should he? He only lived in Offingham.'

They continued looking at the bedrooms. Only the first six were furnished. Two had double beds without any mattresses. One of the other six had some folding chairs stored in it, one a trunk of old clothes, the rest were empty except for their linoleum and the smell of disuse. None of them had a light bulb of above forty watts.

'What's up in the roof?'

'Oh hell!' she said. 'A water tank and a lot of spiders. I wish you knew when you were wasting your time. We'll have to get a ladder from the shed.'

'You know Ove Madsen?' he asked.

'Vaguely.'

'Has Madsen ever stayed here?'

'But he lives in Offingham too,' Wanda said. 'They don't stay here when they're near home.'

'Have you seen him and Teodowicz here together?'

'Yes, perhaps. Once or twice.'

'Were they friendly?'

'They were partners, weren't they? As far as I could see they were good chums.'

90

'How often did they meet Albert here?'

Wanda's face had no expression.

'Who are we talking about now?'

'Let's go and fetch the ladder,' he said.

She followed him without pursuing the question and they went out again into the yard. The ladder was suspended from the brackets of a shelf by pieces of cord which were extravagantly knotted. They untied them, carried the ladder in. The opening in the loft was above the toilets. It was closed by a grimy panel of hardboard which was laced to its frame with spiders' webs. Gently pushed it up, flashed his torch in the loft. He was placed at the junction of the L. The torchlight showed a recession of dusty joists as far as the gable ends, in both directions. Beside him, mounted on cross-pieces of timber, stood a galvanised tank marked by rusty dribbles. He climbed up to it, shone his torch inside. It contained water above a deposit of sludge. He went down.

'That's all,' she said. 'Except the two rooms off the parlour. But if you're not satisfied you can always come back in daylight and root around where you like. I've got nothing to hide here.' The eyes smiled. 'That's the truth,' she said.

'You're not surprised?' he asked.

'What have I got to be surprised about?'

'That I should be searching your premises to find if you are harbouring someone here.'

'Is that what you're doing?'

Gently nodded. 'Have I been looking in drawers and places?'

She screwed up her mouth. 'You're the police. How should I know how your minds work?'

'When did you last see Albert?'

'Albert Sawney?'

'Yes.'

'He came in one night last week.'

'He slept here?'

'Yes.'

'With you?'

'Of course.'

'Did he have Teodowicz and Madsen with him?'

'I don't', she said, 'go in for orgies.'

'Were they with him here any of the time?'

'No. I'm pretty certain Albert doesn't know them.'

'Have you had a message from Albert?'

'No.' She hesitated. 'He just comes in.'

'Do you think he'll get in touch with you?'

'No,' she said. Adding: 'Why should he?'

Gently nodded again. 'I'll just see those other rooms.'

'I've been waiting,' she said. 'One is my bedroom.'

*   *   *

The ladder was returned, the outer door re-bolted. She waited while Gently refilled his pipe and stood again for some moments listening. She showed no impatience. There was no sound in the premises except the tick of a meter, which was mounted over the entry. Outside the plunge of the traffic had grown less continuous but without ever quite giving moments of silence. She watched the smoke eddying from the pipe. She was breathing shallowly but evenly.

'Right,' he said. 'Let's go.'

She turned and preceded him along the corridor. Through the kitchen, into the parlour, to a closed door at the back of the parlour. Behind it was a long narrow room with a further door at the end of it. The narrow room appeared half a junk room but had a divan behind the door.

'Who sleeps here?'

'You may, tonight. Sleeping with me is a figure of speech. I'm fastidious in some things, please understand, and I don't like sharing my bed with people.'

'Did Sawney sleep here?'

'He did if he stayed.'

'What happened with Sawney last week?'

'That was one of the times he stayed.'

'Did he come in his van?'

'No. He had a bike.'

She went straight on into the second room, which was smaller and squarer than the first. It contained a single iron bedstead, a wardrobe, a dressing-table and a chair. Under the bed was a rectangle of linoleum but the boards surrounding it were bare. There was a brush and some cosmetics on the dressing-table, and that was all the room contained. A high small window was ajar. It was curtainless. There was a faint smell of cigarette smoke.

'Do you mind if we have a light on?'

'I don't use a light in here.'

She pointed to an empty socket over the bed. The only light came from the dim bulb next door. He felt in his pocket.

'Cigarette?'

'No, thank you. I don't smoke much.'

She glanced quickly at an ash-tray which stood on the dressing-table. It was empty. She looked away.

'All right, then. Give me one.'

'Sorry . . . I seem to have come out without them.'

She didn't look at him. 'Oh, never mind. I had one here when I was doing my hair.' Then she looked at him. 'Are you through questioning? I didn't really bring you here to smoke.'

Gently puffed, took the chair and reversed it, seated himself on the chair.

'How did you know that Sawney was missing,' he asked, 'if Sawney hasn't been in touch with you?'

'Oh hell,' she said. 'I'm tired of this. Can't you give it a miss for tonight? I want a man, not a policeman. Give me a break, for Christ's sake.'

She breathed hard. She pulled off the dress. She was wearing a pair of drawers under it. She sat on the edge of the bed, leaning towards him, her breasts swelling between her arms.

'Look it over,' she said. 'I'm not voluptuous, but the men go for me. Close the hangar doors for a moment. We can always pick it up later.'

Gently looked. She was not voluptuous. She had narrow thighs and thickish calves. Her fore-arms, too, had a heavy appearance, and the breasts in repose would have been flattened. She looked a little like an athlete, spare, but cast with heavy bone. There was no tenderness about her. Her eroticism was not physical. They stared at each other.

'Well . . . ?' she said. 'Are we going to be friends? I'm not a kid, you understand, I'm well up in the business.'

'You could say that Johnny told you.'

'Blast Johnny. He did, as it happens.'

'Sometimes you don't think very quickly.'

'Put that pipe away,' she said.

Gently puffed.

'You're a bastard,' she said.

They went on staring at each other.

'Look,' she said. 'All right, suspect me. I don't know why or what about. You're a cop, and that's your business. But I'm a woman. And this is mine. I might have had Johnny, you know that, but I froze him off because of you.'

'What was the sweet you gave Tim?'

'Damn Tim and damn all of them.'

'He had egg and chips on Monday night, and some sort of a sweet—trifle, was it?'

'How the hell should I know what he had?'

'Isn't this where he had his meal?'

'He's had meals here, but not on Monday.'

'What time did he get here?'

'Go to hell,' she said.

94

She let herself go backwards across the bed, pulling down the pillow to make her head comfortable. Now her breasts were obviously flat though the nipples were prominently tumescent. She let her feet remain close together. She gave a kick with her hips to settle her position.

'Can't you forget about it?' she asked. 'I'm not holding anything back from you. Tim didn't eat here on the Monday night, I don't know where you got that idea. You're simply on the wrong track altogether. Just because Tim got shot near here. It's a political thing, isn't it?—they wanted Tim to go back to Poland. For Christ's sake be your age, lover. I'm ready for any damned thing at all.'

She stared at him from back on the bed, her eyes closing, her teeth showing. She squared her arms each side of her head and moved her feet a few inches apart. Gently formed a ring of smoke.

'Where's Sawney?' he asked.

She gave a moan. 'Look for the sod.'

'We're doing that,' Gently said.

'So keep on looking for him,' she said.

'We'll do that too,' Gently said. 'But it would save us a lot of sweat if we knew where to look.'

'Ask around, you bastard,' she said. 'You're so damned good at asking questions. I don't know where he'd have gone.'

'This is one likely place.'

She sat up again. 'You lousy slop! Haven't you just been searching everywhere? Nobody lives here with me—I wouldn't have Sawney if he came on his knees. I didn't like him, can't you understand? He was a crude, snidy type. I had him in here when I was stuck for a bloke but that was all—I didn't like him!'

'But he might have come here.'

'He didn't come here!'

'Somebody came in this direction.'

'Oh hell,' she said. 'Hell. Hell. Why did I ever ask you in?'

'That's a question,' he said.

She lay back, moaning. She turned on her side and kicked her legs.

'Get out,' she said from behind her teeth. 'And I hope the next one gives you the pox.'

He rose. He went to look at the ash-tray. He replaced the chair. He went out.

7

Friday August 16th, the day of the inquest on Teodowicz; beginning heavily, dewily, and with the first sun gold. Nothing to mark the day particularly except an incursion of pressmen, and they were barely noticed in the initial bustle of Offingham's High. A number were quartered at the Star. These had noticed Gently's late return. One of the younger ones had sought to question him and had gained experience by doing so. The air was stiller even than yesterday, soft, suspended; the light full of bright glare, penetrating shadows, flattening recessions. The warmth of yesterday lay in the bricks to supplement the warmth of today.

Gently left his car at the Star and walked the two hundred yards to Headquarters. He found Felling in Whitaker's office, and Whitaker absorbing yesterday's developments. A number of leads had come to nothing. Madsen's prints had been found about Teodowicz' flat. Freeman and Rice's search had been abortive. Felling had not found the café where Teodowicz had eaten. The Mini-Minor belonged to Offingham Hire Cars Ltd. and had been returned to them before the police had traced it. The hirer had given the name of Johnson, had not been remembered as wearing dungarees; he was described vaguely as well-spoken, perhaps with an accent, possibly foreign. Felling, after dusting some parts of the car, had concluded that the hirer had worn gloves. Sawney had not been apprehended. There was no word from Empton.

Whitaker got up when Gently entered. 'I'm going to have to congratulate you,' he said. 'Yesterday I was telling you this case hadn't an angle, today you lay the chummie flat on my plate. That's a smart piece of police work, if you don't mind me saying so. That service connection just didn't dawn on us.'

'It would have done,' Gently said, glancing at Felling.

'I'm not sure it would, sir,' Felling said. 'That bottle of cleaning fluid didn't tell me anything. I was out of my depth, so I might as well admit it.'

'But you'd have made inquiries about the gun,' Gently said. 'You'd have got round to Huxford at last. It's too close and handy to overlook. You can see one of the hangars from the lay-by.'

Felling shrugged, stared at nothing.

'We don't mind admitting it,' Whitaker said. 'This is a job where you need a specialist. We haven't had a murder here in living memory. Do you reckon Madsen was in on the racket?'

Gently sat down. 'It seems to follow. We have to accept that he destroyed those records. Though why Teodowicz should keep any records of the racket is one of those curious little points.'

'Well, I got his dabs, sir,' Felling said. 'They were on the poker and on that pin-up.'

'Another curious point,' Gently said. 'I could have sworn Madsen lied to us about that.'

'Yes,' Felling said. 'He was shaky, sir. But there were his dabs, as plain as you could wish.'

'So,' Gently said, 'even a specialist can fall down. I didn't think he had a sense of humour, either.'

'It doesn't matter,' Whitaker said. He was looking pleased. 'We'll see if we can catch up with Madsen later. He couldn't have had anything to do with the killing. If he's a rogue we'll be on to him soon enough. But that bottle was puzzling us. What do you make of the bottle?'

Gently hunched his shoulders. 'That's the third curious

point. Sawney obtains fluid for cleaning a gun, and the fluid turns up in Teodowicz' garage.'

'Perhaps there's nothing to it after all, sir,' Felling said. 'Perhaps Teodowicz got it off him for something else.'

'Or perhaps it was Madsen's,' Whitaker said. 'He may have had a fire-arm, and got rid of it after the killing.'

'Hmn,' Gently said. 'That would be more likely. You wouldn't bother to obtain it unless you had a gun. A pity we couldn't print it.'

'Yes, it was, sir,' Felling said. 'And I reckoned that Madsen knew more about it than he was saying.'

The Town Hall clock chimed a quarter. Felling looked at his wristwatch.

'I'd better be getting down there, sir,' he said to Whitaker. 'I'll need to see one or two people.' To Gently he said: 'Will you be looking in at the inquest, sir? It'll only be the evidence of identification.'

'Yes,' Gently said. 'I'll be looking in. What time is it set for?'

'Eleven hundred hours,' Felling said.

He rose, took his hat. When the door closed Whitaker chuckled.

'Felling's a little peeved by it all,' he said. 'But he's a good fellow. He takes it well. I wonder how his highness from M.I.5 will take it.'

'I don't think he's been told.' Gently had no expression. 'I didn't ask them to pass a message when I was ringing the Yard.'

Whitaker laughed outright. 'You're a bit of a devil. He'll still be chasing this Kasimir fellow. And that must be a frost. You can't have it both ways. With Sawney in the pictrue, Kasimir is out.'

'I wonder,' Gently said.

Whitaker looked at him. 'Oho,' he said.

'I want to talk to Kasimir,' Gently said. 'I don't mind Empton chasing him down.'

Whitaker was silent for a moment. 'You still think there's a connection?' he asked.

'I want to talk to him,' Gently said. 'I don't think he's clear from this at all. And I don't think he's very far away. But I was being slow last night. I'd got the Sawney angle uppermost, I wasn't seeing the picture as a whole. I've been trying to see it since. And I want to talk to Kasimir.'

'Last night,' Whitaker said, puckering his eyes. 'Would that be the fellow whose car you had checked?'

Gently nodded. 'Wearing new dungarees. And hiring a car to go and sit in The Raven. I didn't get a good look at his face and he was gone while I was still trying to place him. But what I saw of him tallied with Empton's photograph. I'm pretty certain he was the man.'

'But what was his interest in The Raven?'

'He probably thinks the same as I do.'

'What do you think?' Whitaker said.

Gently hunched. 'It's not far from the lay-by. And it lies between that and the aerodrome, which is an interesting situation. And the proprietress knew Teodowicz, knows Madsen, knows Sawney. And she knows me. And she's a liar. And she's a very clever woman.'

Whitaker raised his eye-brows. 'What am I to understand by that.'

'It's just for the record,' Gently said. 'I don't want Wanda Lane scared.'

'You want a man there?'

'No. No man. You couldn't do it without her knowing. But you can have a man in the streets looking for Kasimir, and check the hotels and lodging houses.'

'I'll have Freeman do that,' Whitaker said. 'Is there anything else that ought to go on the record?'

Gently looked at him, seemed about to say something, changed his mind, made a slight gesture with his hand. 'There's something really does puzzle me, and that's how the killer got away with it. The appearances are that he ambushed Teodowicz, that is to say, he was waiting hidden in the bushes. Now if he was in the bushes he couldn't see the road, apart from that segment immediately in front of him, yet he seems to have let fly with a prolonged burst as though he were certain there was no other traffic in earshot. This was between one and three a.m. when there is still a trickle of traffic. He couldn't have reckoned on being lucky to such an unlikely extent.'

'Yy—es,' Whitaker said. 'That does seem peculiar. But he certainly used the gun there, we picked up God knows how many shells and bullets. What do you make of it?'

'Hmn,' Gently said. 'He could have had an assistant to watch the traffic.'

'You think he did?'

'No. It would have been too difficult. They could watch the traffic, but they couldn't forecast Teodowicz' arrival. I think it was something else . . . I think we may have under-estimated the cunning of this chummie.'

'In what way?'

Gently said: 'Information. Would you know Baddesley pretty well?'

'I was born and brought up there,' Whitaker said. 'How does Baddesley come into it?'

'Is the station in the middle of the town?'

'No, about half a mile outside it. Baddesley is only a town by courtesy title—not important enough to bend the main line for.'

'Where is the car park with reference to the station?'

'It's round at the back. You go under a bridge.'

'Any lights there? Any attendant?'

Whitaker shook his head. 'It's just the corner of a field.'

'Yes,' Gently said. 'That fits in. Sawney's van was found there, remember. And the service police elicited that some airmen were catching early trains, though they couldn't get Sawney identified—there are several R.A.F. stations in the district. But his van was there, that's hard fact. Sawney went there that night.'

He frowned at Whitaker. Whitaker watched him.

'Let's try it this way,' he said. 'Sawney drives to Baddesley Station. He has a way to make Teodowicz meet him there— proof that he was in the racket with him, perhaps: any way, he gets him there. And when he arrives Sawney contrives to attack him and either kills him or knocks him out, then he puts the body in the back of Teodowicz' van and drives it along to the lay-by. Now the problem is much simpler. Sawney can bide his time for a break in the traffic. Then he fires his burst into Teodowicz, part of it from the bushes to suggest an ambush, and escapes over the fields, leaving a trail of misdirection behind him. Very roughly, that fits the facts.'

'Yes,' Whitaker said. 'Nothing overlooks the car park. But if it's as you say, why did Sawney bother to use the Sten gun—if Teodowicz was dead, where was the point?'

'He might not have been dead,' Gently said. 'Sawney wouldn't have risked a shot near the station. And then when he did open up, all his lust for vengeance went into it.' He grinned at Whitaker. 'Or something,' he said. 'I was never much good at spinning a theory. I'm just trying to get a shape that fits the facts where it touches.'

'Oh yes, it fits,' Whitaker said.

'If one could only believe in it. But it calls for a surprising amount of calculation from a man whose first object is to kill. He learns he's betrayed, he grabs a gun, he rushes off to exact vengeance, and then he embarks on a curious plan of cool-headed misdirection. And yet it worked something like that, because the facts require it. The facts we know, that is. It could be we're lacking a key part.'

'Such as Kasimir,' Whitaker said.

Gently nodded. 'He could be that factor. Until we know where he fits, there's a blur in the focus.'

'You're thinking he maybe took a hand in it.'

'I think he's still playing his cards. But what his game is I can't fathom. And maybe Empton can tell us that.'

'Empton,' Whitaker said. 'I can't get over him. I didn't know blokes like him existed.'

'Complete with Jaguar,' Gently said.

The Town Hall clock struck another quarter.

*   *   *

He walked down the High to the Coroner's Court, which was situated across a small public garden at the back of the Town Hall. The public garden was enclosed by the high walls of surrounding buildings and had a mean, sunless look, with moss growing in the lozenges of thin grass. The Coroner's Court filled one side of it, a single-storey building of damp brick. A mortuary was attached to it on the left and both bore the date: 1887. People stood about the garden. One or two were wearing mourning. A spruce, plump man moved among them with a subdued, wistful smile. He had a supply of cards which he was discreetly offering. At the door of the court stood two uniformed constables. They touched their helmets as Gently approached. One of them said:

'I think you're a bit late, sir.'

Gently checked. 'How do you mean?'

'The inquest, sir. It'll be about over. It's been going on for half an hour.'

'Isn't it at eleven?'

'Half-past ten, sir.' The constable looked mildly wondering.

'I was told eleven.'

103

'No sir. Half-past ten. They naturally put it at the top of the list.'

As he was speaking a door near them opened and a number of the pressmen began to push out. They were not in a hurry, began lighting cigarettes, seemed only to wake up when they spotted Gently.

'Any statement for us yet?'

'No statement.'

'Is Sawney in this?'

'Who's Sawney?'

'The bloke whose picture we're running.'

'You'll get a statement from H.Q.'

He shoved in at the door against the current of people who were trying to get out. He found himself at the public end of the court, which was long, low and badly lit. Only the local man remained at the press tables and the public gallery was on its feet. Madsen, wearing a cheap but neat blue suit, stood at the bench saying something to the coroner. Felling stood not far behind him, looking sullen. The coroner was scribbling on a piece of paper. He nodded twice and handed the paper to Madsen, Madsen glanced fearfully at Felling, left the court. Felling saw Gently, came down to meet him.

'There's been some funny business, sir,' he muttered. 'It's lucky I came down here early. The inquest wasn't at eleven at all.'

'What made you think it was at eleven?'

'That's where the funny business comes in, sir. Somebody rang my flat during breakfast this morning to say the inquest had been put back till eleven. Said he was calling from the Coroner's office.'

'Did he identify himself?'

'Yes sir. Said he was the Coroner's clerk. And his voice didn't sound unlike Mr. Jimpson's.'

'Which is Mr. Jimpson?'

'That gentleman there, sir.'

'Have you asked him about it?'

'I was just going to tackle him, sir.'

Gently went up to Jimpson, who was now going over a typewritten sheet with the Coroner; a small-featured man with aggressive eyes and close-cropped silver grey hair. He turned sharply at Gently's approach.

'Mr. Jimpson?'

'That's me, sir.'

'Did you ring Sergeant Felling's flat this morning to tell him that the inquest had been put back till eleven?'

Jimpson stared frostily at Gently.

'No sir. I did not.'

'Would any of your staff have done that?'

'They would not. Why should they?'

'Has the time set for the inquest been changed at any point?'

'No sir. At no point.'

'Thank you, Mr. Jimpson,' Gently said.

Jimpson said nothing, turned back to the Coroner.

Felling shook his head, looked stupid. 'I just don't get this at all, sir,' he said.

'Neither do I,' Gently said. 'There doesn't seem to have been any object in it. Where would you have been, if you hadn't arrived here?'

'Up at Headquarters, sir, preparing to come.'

'Which would have meant a delay of five minutes when you were inquired for, and nothing more.' Gently shrugged. 'Could it have been a joke?'

Felling looked ugly. 'It better hadn't have been, sir.'

'Was there anything familiar about the voice?'

'Not that I remember, sir. I took it for Mr. Jimpson's.'

'No foreign intonation.'

'No sir,' Felling said. 'Just short and sharp, just the way he always speaks.'

Gently nodded slowly. 'Well . . . you were here on time, whatever the object might have been. Everything went smoothly, did it—nothing unexpected turned up?'

'Nothing at all, sir,' Felling said. 'It was just identification and a postponement.'

'What was Madsen saying to the Coroner?'

'Madsen . . . ?'

'Just now. As I came in.'

'Oh that—it was about the burial certificate,' Felling said. 'Madsen wants to bury him out of town. He's getting worried, sir, about the publicity. The reporters have been giving him a rough passage. He asked if he could have the funeral at the Westlow Chapel, which is a couple of miles out of Offingham. I didn't think we had any objection.'

'He won't fool anybody,' Gently said. 'When is this funeral?'

'I think it's later today, sir, if Madsen can put the arrangements through.'

'It'll be his best chance,' Gently said. Suddenly he turned to look down the court. From the dimness of the public gallery at the other end something had faintly, briefly flashed. There was a small commotion in the gallery. A man was squeezing his way towards the door. He wore a dark suit and carried a black trilby and moved sideways, with his back to the court. Gently grabbed Felling's arm.

'Come on! I want that man detained.'

'Who . . . which . . . ?' Felling gabbled.

The man reached the door. He had begun to run.

*   *   *

Outside the bright sun put Gently at fault for a moment. He stood blinking, looking about the garden, while Felling rushed up behind him.

'Who is it sir?'

'Bring those constables!'

Felling shouted instructions to the two men.

Gently caught a quick movement across the garden and set off running towards one of the gates. The street outside was Bullock Street, leading from the Market Place towards the river; a narrow street of slovenly houses with many lane-turnings and yards. The man had gone towards the river. He had disappeared from the street when Gently reached it. There were parked cars in the street, but in that direction, few people. Gently ran on to the first turning. It was a long, empty service lane. He ran to the second. It was a cul-de-sac. An errand boy was cycling slowly down it.

'Has a man come this way?' Gently bawled.

'There's a bloke ran across the road.'

'Which way?'

'Down Boulting Lane.'

A plate over a turning opposite read: Boulting Lane.

Gently crossed over, ran into the lane. Felling and the constables followed after him. The lane slanted downhill between irregular tarred walls of old house-ends, warehouses, scrap-yards. Half-way down it a turn revealed a parked truck on to which two men were loading baled waste-paper. They stared at Gently, stopped loading the truck.

'Has a man come by here?' Gently panted.

'What sort of a man?'

'Any sort of a man!'

'Not in the last ten minutes,' said the speaker. 'We haven't seen nobody, have we, Ted?'

'No,' Ted said. 'We haven't seen nobody.'

Gently rounded on Felling and the constables. 'One of you run back to the top of the lane. Stop anybody entering or going out. We're looking for a man of medium build, about forty, darkish colouring, dark grey lounge suit, black trilby, probably speaks with a slight accent. Detain him by force if necessary.'

The younger constable sprinted back up the lane.

'You stay here,' Gently said to the other man. 'Same instructions. Stop anyone coming or going.'

He paused a moment to get his wind, watched while the younger constable reached his station. Then he said to Felling: 'You take that side. We'll work up the lane and flush him out.'

'Is it this Kasimir bloke?' Felling breathed.

'We'll see when we get him,' Gently said. 'Take your time and search thoroughly, and don't use kid gloves if you tangle with him.'

'I don't own kid gloves,' Felling said. 'A chummie comes quiet or a chummie is carried.'

They began to search. There were seven entries off the lane. They served a metal scrap-yard, a wholesale fruit warehouse, a cardboard-box manufacturer's warehouse, a paint store, a tyre store, a sign-writer's and a building contractor's. In six of these seven premises men were working. They gladly left off working to answer questions and watch. They had not seen a man running, had not admitted any stranger. They pointed out places where he might have hid. He was in none of those places. At the top and bottom of the stretch of lane the two constables rocked slowly on their heels. There remained the metal scrap-yard with its wire-mesh gates, which were ten feet high. Felling frowned at the gates.

'It's here or nowhere, sir,' he said. 'But chummie was a bit of a Spring-heeled Jack if he sailed over those gates.'

'Who has the keys to these?' Gently asked.

'They'll be in Cambridge,' said one of the watchers. 'Dukey and Son, that's who owns it. They've got a big place in Cambridge.'

'A big help,' Felling said. 'A big help.'

Gently went to the gates, began examining the mesh. The mesh was galvanized but was beginning to rust and at one place the rust had been chafed and showed orange. He examined the mesh a little higher. He found another chafed spot. The mesh was two-and-a-half inch mesh into which a toe could not be effectively inserted. He stood back, ran an eye over the watchers.

'You,' he said to a slim youth in a boiler suit. The youth edged forward. 'Could you climb those gates?'

'Reckon I could,' the youth said. 'Give me time.'

'You haven't got time,' Gently said. 'You're in a hurry. You're belting down the lane with the cops behind you and you see these gates and you want to get over them.'

The youth looked at the gates, narrowing his eyes. 'Reckon I could,' he said.

'Right,' Gently said. 'Show me. Go up the lane and take a run at them.'

The youth stared a little, then spit on his hands and stalked some paces up the lane. He came flying back, threw himself at the gates, scrabbled desperately at the mesh and hauled himself up. He waved some bleeding fingers at Gently.

'Nothing to it,' he said.

'The saucy young devil!' Felling said. 'Those gates are supposed to be prowler-proof.'

'Thanks,' Gently said. 'You did that nicely. You'd better come down and have the cuts seen to. And perhaps some of you will find us a couple of ladders so we don't have to tackle the gates the hard way.'

The youth came down and stood sucking his fingers. Two ladders were fetched from the contractor's yard. Since the gates were on the side which Felling had been searching he took the initiative in climbing over. But he had barely got to the top when Gently said 'Hold it!' and the watchers went quiet. Felling stared into the yard. A figure had appeared there. It stood across by the far wall and was brushing the dust from its grey lounge suit.

*   *   *

'You over there!' Gently shouted.

The man looked towards them, kept dusting himself. He was standing at the foot of a mound of old gas cookers which may have been thirty feet high. The suit fitted him very well and showed that he had a neat, athletic figure, and as his hands moved the sun glinted from the big stone of his ring. Finally he picked up his hat and dusted that too, settled it squarely on his head. He looked at his hands, flexed the fingers. He began to walk towards the gates.

He came up to the gates. He stood looking through them at Gently. He had walked with a very slight limp. He had dark hair and black-brown eyes and wide cheek-bones and a narrow chin. The chin was not a receding chin. The mouth was thin and the corners drooped. The nose was handsome and large. He had no moustache. His tie was not a bow tie. He stood looking through the meshes at Gently. His eyes were steady. But his hands trembled.

'What's your name?' Gently asked.

His lips opened, then he said: 'Campbell.'

'Donald Campbell?'

'Campbell,' he said.

'A Scotsman, are you?'

'That is right. A Scotsman.'

'Have you any proof of identity?'

'I am Campbell,' he said.

'What were you doing in this yard?'

He shook his head, saying nothing.

'Good,' Gently said. 'So have you any objection to accompanying me to the police station?'

'No,' he said, 'of course. No objection.'

'Then perhaps you'll climb over that gate.'

He went to the ladder which was placed his side and mounted it with quick, jerky movements. Felling came down the other ladder and the man stepped over to it and descended into the lane. He looked at nobody. He straightened his suit, felt for the brim of his hat. Then he was suddenly bolting up the lane, slipping by Felling's clumsy lunge for him.

'Stop that bastard!' Felling roared.

The constable at the top held out clutching hands. The man raced towards him till he was a dozen yards short, then seemed to give up the idea, checked, came to a stand. Felling and the constable closed in on him. Before they could touch him he was bolting again. But this time Felling managed to kick his heels together. He went to the ground. They grabbed him and held him.

'You treacherous so-and-so!' Felling was panting. 'I'll teach you to play that kind of trick.'

He was twisting the arm of the man behind him. The man had gone white. His eyes were closed and squinting.

'Let him get up,' Gently said.

'The cunning bastard!' Felling panted.

'Let him get up all the same,' Gently said.

Felling yanked the man to his feet. He and the constable held him. The man sagged against them, pale, breathing hard. He opened his eyes. He stared fearfully at Gently.

'You value you liberty,' Gently said.

The corners of the mouth pulled down, trembled.

'All right,' Gently said. 'Let's get him to the station.'

The constable picked up the man's hat. They took him away.

'What's your name?'

'I am Campbell.'

'Show me your wallet.'

The man produced it. A stiff, pigskin wallet, nearly new, very slim. It contained fourteen one pound notes and two ten shilling notes but nothing else. The notes were new notes with consecutive numbers, except the two ten shillings.

'Where's your driving licence?'

'It is not with me.'

'Where is it?'

He shook his head.

'Put the contents of your pockets on the desk.'

He emptied his pockets. He made a neat pile.

The pile consisted of five half-crowns, a florin, two six-pences, two threepenny pieces, five pennies, three halfpennies, a cheap pen-knife, a ball pen, a clean handkerchief, a packet of Chesterfield cigarettes, a box of Swan matches, a Yale key on a ring, and a silver charm shaped like a rabbit's foot, also attached to the ring.

'What's the key for?'

'It is for my flat.'

'What's the address of it?'

He shook his head.

'Don't you know where you come from?'

'Yes,' he said.

'Is it far from West Hampstead?'

He sat still.

'What are your Christian names?'

'I am Campbell.'

'Jan Campbell?'

'Yes, John.'

'I said Jan.'

'John,' he said. 'I am always called John.'

'Not Jan?'

'No. Not Jan.'

'Jan Campbell?'

The mouth drooped.

'All right,' Gently said. 'You can smoke, Jan. Have a cigarette, Jan. Relax, Jan.'

'I do not want to smoke now,' the man said.

'Just as you like, Jan.'

He sat still.

Felling, Whitaker sat in the office, Whitaker beside Gently and Felling near the door. Felling had his arms folded, looked through the window. Whitaker's pale eyes went from Gently to the man. Whitaker was frowning as though trying and wanting to understand. He had a large face. His face looked childish. Behind it he was shrewd. Felling's eyes looked vacant. The man sat tensely. His eyes never left Gently. Gently was removing the photograph of Jan Kasimir from its file. He propped it up. He looked at the man.

'When did you shave your moustache, Jan?'

'I have not a moustache.'

'Not since when?'

He shook his head.

'You had one there, Jan.'

'My name is John.'

'Jan. That's what it says.'

'I don't know what it says.'

'It says Jan Kasimir.'

'I am Campbell.'

'Jan Kasimir.'

'Campbell.'

Gently shrugged. 'It's quite a good photograph of you, Jan,' he said. 'Don't you like it?'

'Is not of me.'

'Perhaps you don't like the moustache?'

'I have not ever a moustache.'

'Oh, I think it was a nice touch. When did you shave it?'

His knuckles were white.

'Before you saw Teodowicz?'

'Who is Teodowicz?'

'The man whose inquest you went to, Jan.'

'I do not know him.'

'Your fellow-countryman.'

'I am Scotsman.'

'Timoshenko Teodowicz.'

'No,' the man said. 'I do not know him. I do not know anything about Teodowicz.'

'Don't you read the papers?'

He sat still. He bit his lips together very hard.

'And Teodowicz is dead,' Gently said. 'And the way he died wasn't pretty, Jan. There was nothing parsimoniously Scottish about the number of bullets that went into him. Over two hundred of them, did you know that? Somebody stood there pumping them into him. Not long after you'd been to see him. The man whose inquest you attended today.'

He sat still.

'Unpleasant,' Gently said. 'Haven't you any comment to make, Jan?'

The lips bit tighter.

'A pity,' Gently said. 'Somebody is going to hang for Teodowicz, Jan.'

The man was trembling. He leaned forward. His eyes stretched wide, showing rings of white. '*Hypocrite!*' he screamed at Gently. He crumbled in the chair. He began to cry.

'Well,' Gently said. 'A comment after all. Why am I a hypocrite, Jan?'

The man was sobbing to himself words not in English. He didn't pay any more attention to Gently.

Whitaker flinched, looked unhappy, asked: 'What are we going to do about him?'

Gently watched the man crying. He had covered his face with his hands. The hands were pale hands and the fingers were sensitive. They too had been bleeding. The blood had dried on the fingers.

Gently chucked his head. 'We'll have to unleash Empton. I'm afraid we've strayed into his department.'

'Empton,' Whitaker said.

Gently picked up the phone. The man continued to cry, Felling to stare through the window.

*   *   *

Friday August 16th in a small town, in a small country, in a small world, in a large universe, Friday August 16th. A certain point in space-time with a very local description, un-accepted as an event by the electronic expression containing it. Perhaps emotion, no more, an alien wanderer in the curva-tures; the burden carried by those other lonely aliens, men. Giving them local habitation where they were strangers gone foreign, a detailed assurance of identification, a comfortable shadow on their blank chart. Friday August 16th in a small town, in a small country. A point negligible in space-time. A man crying. Other men.

*   *   *

The door opened to admit Empton. He didn't come into the room immediately. He stood in the doorway, hand on the knob, peering at the man who sat drooped in his chair. Empton's blue eyes didn't flicker and he stood as still as the door. He didn't look anywhere except at the man. Finally, his teeth began to show.

'Little Jan!' he said softly. 'We wondered where you'd got to, little Jan.'

He closed the door without a sound, and reaching behind him, shot the snack.

The man twisted round at the sound of Empton's voice, crouched a little, didn't say anything. Whitaker rose, pushing his chair back clumsily. Empton came across the room.

'Is he the—one?' Whitaker asked.

'But of course, old man,' Empton said. 'This is little Jan, the West Hampstead instrument-maker. We've met before, haven't we Jan?'

'My name—' the man began.

'Oh, don't lets be formal, old fellow,' said Empton. 'You're with friends, don't you remember? My little visit and advice I gave you?' He ran the tips of his fingers over his knuckles. Kasimir kept his eye on the knuckles. 'I sometimes look in on these chaps,' Empton said, 'when they first arrive here. A purely courtesy call. What's he been telling you?'

'Nothing,' Gently said.

Empton showed his teeth. 'They don't,' he said. 'That's one of the oddities of the profession, old man. There's really only two ways of getting anything out of them.'

'What's the other way?' Gently said.

'Money,' Empton said. 'And we'll try that first. Purely out of deference to bourgeois prejudices. I don't think it will work, not in the present company. I think he killed Teodowicz. I think your presence will be inhibiting.'

'I think it probably will,' Gently said. 'So I'll stay here.'

'Just as you like,' Empton said. 'It doesn't matter. If you took him to court you'd never get a conviction.'

He looked round the office, picked up the chair Felling had

116

used, placed it so he sat opposite to Kasimir with their knees nearly touching. He flicked Kasimir's chin. Kasimir jerked his head back. Empton leaned forward slightly, stared hard, flicked him again. Whitaker seated himself uneasily. He sent glances at Gently. Gently sat with half-closed eyes, hunching back in his chair.

'Little Jan,' Empton said.

Kasimir sat very straight.

'Little Jan,' Empton said, 'you've got something we want. We're going to have it, little Jan, and you know we're going to have it. That's the situation, little Jan. I think you appreciate it, don't you?'

He flicked. Kasimir winced, didn't try to avoid it.

'Yes,' Empton said. 'You're a man of intelligence, you appreciate the situation. We know too much to be played with, Jan, and I'm sure you won't waste our time by trying it. You're going to give us what we want, Jan, because there's no other way out. You're going to co-operate, Jan. You're going to tell us everything, Jan.'

He flicked.

'Now', he said. 'We're going to be generous with you, Jan. We could hang you, Jan. You know that? We could put up a case that would hang you for certain. And you've come such a long way, Jan, you've been through so much, Jan, it would be a pity, wouldn't it, Jan, if we had to hang you at the end of it. All strapped up with a hood over your face. Such a long way from Poland. It isn't nice, Jan. Not being hung. You wouldn't want us to do that, would you?'

He flicked twice at Kasimir's throat. Kasimir gasped, didn't move.

'And we don't want to do it, Jan,' Empton said. 'We're soft-hearted. It would grieve us. And you're a useful man in your way, Jan, it would be a waste to hang you. So we're going to be generous with you, Jan. We're not going to

117

hang you, Jan, unless we have to. We're going to be terribly nice and English, and hope that you'll be nice to us. You're in a free country, Jan, you know that?'

He flicked.

'You know that?' he repeated.

Kasimir swallowed, nodded his head.

'Yes,' Empton said. 'A free country.' He touched his knuckles with his fingers. 'And we hope that you'll be nice to us, just like one Englishman to another. And useful, Jan, to your new country. Co-operative, Jan. Patriotic, Jan. And not too bloody expensive, Jan. Remembering how easily we could hang you. The taxpayers pay their money grudgingly. We have to be sparing of it, Jan.' He flicked Jan. 'How much do you want?'

Kasimir didn't move a muscle.

Empton flicked. 'You heard me, Jan?'

Kasimir breathed hard, didn't speak.

Empton laid his fist on Kasimir's chin and pushed Kasimir's head first one way, then the other.

'Little Jan,' he said. 'How much?'

Kasimir stared at him. He said nothing.

'Perhaps little Jan is afraid,' Empton said. 'Perhaps he doesn't trust us with his secrets. Thinks if he told us how he killed Teodowicz we might write it down and use it as evidence. But that's because little Jan is a wog. He doesn't understand our English justice. He doesn't know that a confession of murder obtained by a bribe is inadmissable. But he's hearing it now, isn't he, Jan?' Empton gave Kasimir a double slap. 'And he knows he can deal, doesn't he, Jan?' Empton feinted a slap, let his hand fall. 'So what's the price, little Jan?'

Kasimir closed his eyes, rocked a little.

'A couple of thou?' Empton said. 'Don't go to sleep, Jan. I might have to wake you.'

'I did not kill him,' Kasimir said huskily. 'You know about that. It is not me.'

'Eloquence,' Empton said, slapping him. 'Little Jan has got a tongue.'

'I did not kill him,' Kasimir said. 'I will not confess. I did not kill him.'

'I'll make it three thousand,' Empton said.

'No,' Kasimir said. 'Was not me.'

Empton slapped him. 'Don't push your market.' He slapped him again. 'Three and a half.'

'No. No.'

Empton paused. 'Just what have you got to sell us?' he asked. 'Who was Teodowicz?'

'I don't know.'

'Four thou.'

'Is no good,' Kasimir said.

Empton slapped him. 'Five thou.'

'No,' Kasimir said. 'I will not confess.'

'What's the figure?'

Kasimir said nothing. Empton slapped him. Kasimir still said nothing.

'So it's something big,' Empton said. 'Or you think it is, little Jan. And you're not going to muck it away because you think we can't stick you with the killing. But you're wrong there, little Jan. We can fix you up all right. And we don't have to put in a confession which the judge would sling straight back at us.' He eased away from Kasimir. 'We've got you taped, little Jan,' he said. 'You received instructions to kill Teodowicz. We pay money. We get info.'

'No!' Kasimir said.

'Oh yes,' Empton said. 'You're a little green in the racket, aren't you? There's plenty of double-selling goes on among the ranks of Tuscany, you know. And you've been sold. Right up the Volga. You were sent here to kill him, little

Jan. You took a week off from making instruments and you came here, and you killed Teodowicz.'

Empton leant forward casually, gave Kasimir a double slap.

'Six thou,' he said. 'We'll find a level of interest somewhere.'

Kasimir sat up even straighter. 'That is a lie!' he cried passionately.

Empton slapped him several times.

'Naughty,' he said. 'Don't call me a liar.'

'But it is a lie. I was not sent to kill him!'

'Seven thousand?' Empton said.

'And I shall never, never, confess it!'

Empton hit him in the mouth.

'I don't know why I bother,' he said. 'This is only to satisfy bourgeois prejudice. If we leak some info in the right direction, *you'll* get no more letters out of Poland.'

Kasimir sprang up. 'Swine!' he screamed. Empton punched him in the stomach.

'Don't get hysterical, Jan,' he said. 'It isn't British. Don't do it.'

Kasimir fell back in the chair, gasping, sobbing, clutching his stomach. Empton watched him. He turned to Whitaker.

'Sorry to worry you, old man,' he said.

'I think that's enough of that,' Whitaker said.

'Damned un-bourgeois,' Empton said. 'But I've probably made my point now.'

'I think that's enough of it,' Whitaker said.

Kasimir sobbed. His mouth was bleeding. He didn't try to cover his face. He sat holding his stomach and crying, like any child might cry.

'Well, well,' Empton said. 'Well, well, little Jan. Did you cry when you shot Teodowicz, or did you just close your eyes?'

'Swine, swine,' Kasimir sobbed.

'Why was he killed, little Jan?'

'It is you who kill him,' Kasimir sobbed. 'The British police. You kill Teodowicz.'

'Dear me,' Empton said. 'This is doing us too much honour. Why should we kill Teodowicz, when you can think up an answer?'

'Because we talk to him,' Kasimir sobbed. 'Because we ask him to go back. So you kill him, that is why. To make it seem that we kill people.'

'How extraordinary,' Empton said. 'It sounds almost strange enough to be true.'

'And you do kill him!' Kasimir sobbed. 'It is not us. It is *you*.'

Empton stared at him for some moments. 'No,' he said. 'It's too simple. Think again, little Jan. I don't think we can quite swallow that one.'

'Yes,' Kasimir sobbed, 'yes. It is you who have done that. That is why I have to come back, to find out who has done the killing. And now I know. It is you. And you want that I shall confess. And I never, never shall confess. It is the British police who kill Teodowicz!'

'Better and better,' Empton said. 'Who is your contact man, Jan?'

'How should I know who he is—twice, only, I have seen him.'

'What do they call him?' Empton said.

'I do not know what they call him.'

'Is he tall, short, fat, thin?'

'He is tall man, not fat.'

'A Pole, is he?'

'Yes,' Kasimir sobbed.

'And that's all the description you can give us?'

'He comes from the Embassy!' Kasimir sobbed. 'He is man like you. But he is a Pole.'

*   *   *

Empton's teeth appeared very slowly. 'A man like me, Jan,' he said. 'We're getting compliments thick and fast now you're opening your mouth a little. Is it Razek?'

'I do not know.'

'A man with grey eyes and a cheek scar.'

'I do not know . . . yes, a scar.'

'Speaks slowly. Doesn't look at you.'

'Yes,' Kasimir said. 'That is the man.'

'Wears light grey suits, pale ties.'

'Yes, a light grey suit,' Kasimir said. 'That is the man. Speaks slowly.'

'Well, well,' Empton said. 'So this is one of Razek's projects. And he's a man like me, is he, Jan? That's more of a compliment than you're aware of. Razek,' he said to Whitaker, 'is an old acquaintance of mine. Rule Britannia to one side, I'm a great admirer of Razek's. That makes little Jan almost a friend. I'm sure we ought to do some business. I'm sure it would hurt Razek's feelings if we were crude enough to deport little Jan.' He flicked Kasimir affectionately. 'Now see here, Jan,' he said. 'Let's get together on this like pals instead of playing it tough with each other.'

'I have told you about it,' Kasimir said.

'Yes,' Empton said. 'But not enough. Cards on the table, Jan, old fellow, then we'll see about a deal. You aren't in this for love, I know, and we don't expect you to be. There's some ready money sitting in my car and it was signed out especially for little Jan. Now—why did Teodowicz have to die?'

Kasimir moaned, covered his face.

'I'm not asking who killed him,' Empton said. 'That's something we'll leave between you and Razek. These things happen. You didn't want to do it. You had pressure put on you, I know about that. And Razek had pressure put on him too, he isn't a man who kills for policy. But he'd give you a hint of why you were doing it, and it's that hint I'm ready to pay for. This is business, little Jan. You don't have to fence any longer.'

'I will not confess,' Kasimir said. He said it between his teeth. 'I will not confess.'

'Jan,' Empton said. 'You play ball with me and I'll play ball with you. You won't be touched if you co-operate, you'll just get your money, that's all. You'll go back to West Hampstead and you'll report to Razek that we're off the scent—he'll believe it, I'll drop some info—and he'll never know about the deal. Then I'll give you a man you can contact when something fresh turns up, and you'll be paid pretty well, Jan. We aren't mean with our agents.'

Kasimir sobbed.

'Jan,' Empton said. 'You aren't listening, Jan.'

'I will not confess,' Kasimir said.

Empton struck him in the face.

'Here,' Whitaker said. 'That's enough. I'm not going to permit that sort of thing.'

'Bloody wogs,' Empton said. 'He'll talk.'

'I won't have it,' Whitaker said.

'I'll take him back with me,' Empton said. 'He'll talk. A couple of days will make him vocal.'

Gently said: 'He walks out of that door unless you've a charge to hang on him.'

Empton turned to look at Gently. He stared hard, showed the teeth. 'Bless my soul, old man,' he said. 'English justice in person. You want to be technical? I'll be technical. I've got a charge tucked up my sleeve for him. He's an alien, you know, and you heard what he admitted to us. He's been in touch with a foreign power.'

'They've been in touch with him,' Gently said. 'He seems to have been under some duress.'

'The mere spirit,' Empton said. 'You asked for the letter,

I've given it to you. And don't forget that Teodowicz was murdered, however venial the act may seem. I think the law has a hold on Jan, if Jan has a hold on the law.'

'Jan,' Gently said, 'will you talk to me now?'

'I won't confess,' Kasimir whispered.

'I'm not asking you to confess,' Gently said. 'I'd just like you to explain what you told us. It wasn't us who killed Teodowicz, and we're not trying to find a scapegoat. But we have to understand how you came into it. That seems to have a bearing on Teodowicz' death. Won't you tell me about that?'

'I have told you this,' Kasimir said. He began crying again, with a helpless bitterness. Empton sighed, got up, walked over to the window.

'Jan,' Gently said.

Kasimir sobbed. His face was twisted and blotched with tears.

'Jan.'

'I have told you. . . .'

'It's important, Jan.'

'I have told you . . . I go to speak to him.' He faced Gently, his eyes glazed. 'I am not a criminal,' he said. 'I am a decent person, you understand . . .? I want to live like a decent person.'

'Tell me, Jan,' Gently said.

'And I'm not a coward!' Kasimir sobbed. 'I was in the Resistance, I fought the Germans, I have been tortured, sentenced to death . . . I am not a coward, you understand? They broke my leg . . . I am not a coward.'

'Tell me what happened,' Gently said.

'And I am not a traitor,' Kasimir sobbed. 'I leave Poland, but I am not a traitor. I love Poland very much. I am not a traitor to Poland. I think it is good, much that they do there. But me, I have said too many things, I have to leave, I have to come here . . . and I do not have any illusions about your country, I think only you let me live decent. You understand? I want to live decent, I have all that I can take. . . .' He broke down again. 'I am not a traitor. . . .'

'Go on, Jan,' Gently said.

'I love Poland,' he sobbed. 'I love my mother and my sister.'

'They're still in Poland?'

'Yes . . . still in Poland.'

'And that was the pressure they put on you?'

Kasimir nodded. 'This man . . . he knows my mother and sister by name. He does not threaten me, nothing like that. Just ask me how they are getting on. . . .'

'What had you to do?' Gently said.

'To talk to Teodowicz, this is all. To make him see it is right for him to go back, stand trial. . . .'

'Not to threaten him?'

'No . . . this is true! I have to appeal to him to go back. It is good if he do this, you understand? He would not get a heavy sentence.'

'And you talked to Teodowicz.'

'Yes, of course. I cannot do anything else.'

'How did he take it?'

'He does not like it . . . is a big shock, I think. All this time he has been forgotten, thinks he has done with all that. Then I talk to him.' Kasimir gulped. 'I did not want to do that.'

'Was he difficult?'

'No, not difficult . . . he knows I could not help coming. He is shocked, first of all . . . doesn't know what to do about it. He asks me if he is threatened. I tell him no, no threats. What will happen, he says, if I take no notice. I do not know what to tell him. He keeps walking up and down, up and down, like an animal.'

'Did he make his mind up?'

'No. He must have time, he says. I must come back in a few days, then he will know what to tell me.'

'What did you do?'

'I stop here. I have to go back with an answer. I tell him where he can find me so he can talk to me again.'

'I see,' Gently said. He sat some moments frowning at the desk. 'What were you doing during that time—two or three days, it would be?'

Kasimir gave a little shrug. 'It is very dull. I visit Cambridge I have a friend there, a college professor, he will tell you it is true. Mathias Lukov, that is his name. He is in the telephone directory.'

'You were in Cambridge on Monday?'

'Yes. I am sleeping here, you understand. On Monday we go to the Arts Theatre, a first night, "The Italian Straw Hat". I have a hire car, you see, I come back quite late.'

'How late?'

'Oh, after midnight. We had some supper in Lukov's rooms.'

'You can prove it?'

'But yes. There is Lukov, also his friends. It is a small party, six or seven. I am not back here till perhaps two o'clock.'

'Go on,' Gently said. 'How did you learn that Teodowicz was dead?'

'It is in the news,' Kasimir said. 'The B.B.C., Tuesday morning. I hear it at breakfast where I am staying. I am flabbergasted to hear this. If he had shot himself I could understand, but he could not have shot himself like that. I go back to London straight away and get in touch with this man, he says the British police must have done it to give our government a bad name. He is very surprised too, cannot understand at all. I must return to Offingham, he tells me, try to find out the truth about it.'

'What did you find out?' Gently asked.

Kasimir shrugged again. 'I am a poor detective. I think that woman have something to do with it, the one you talk to at the café.'

Gently nodded. 'But now you think we did it?'

Kasimir said nothing, glanced at Empton's back.

'You don't really believe that,' Gently said. 'Just as I don't believe you did it, either.'

Kasimir looked at him. 'You know . . .?' He hesitated.

'I'm getting a rough idea,' Gently said.

'It is difficult,' Kasimir said slowly. 'Very difficult. I think perhaps you are a good detective.'

'You'll be seeing this man again—Mr. Razek?'

Kasimir glanced at Empton again. 'Yes. I have appointment.'

'You'd better tell him you've talked to us about it,' Gently said. 'And that at the moment it looks to us like a simple criminal job. It may or may not concern some other nationals, but we don't regard it primarily as a political killing. We're as anxious as he is, you can tell him, to avoid giving this case a political colouring.'

'I will tell him,' Kasimir said. 'I will return today and tell him.'

Empton turned from the window. 'How nice,' he said. 'How terribly nice. Little Jan and English justice settling their differences like gentlemen. What a pity we haven't got it on tape to give them a belly laugh in the Kremlin.' He showed his teeth, came into the room. 'Sad,' he said, 'I must break up the act. But I belong to a different school of thought and suffer from a chronically reluctant gullet. Little Jan isn't sliding off yet, for all his cultivated wog-pals in Cambridge.'

'I think he is,' Gently said.

'Decent of you, old man,' Empton said. 'But I've a charge to prefer, don't you remember? Are you up to charging someone yet, old man?'

'Oh yes,' Gently said. 'Ever since last night.'

'A parking offence?' Empton said.

'No, murder,' Gently said. 'This is a murder case. Haven't you seen the newspapers lately?'

He took a newspaper out of his pocket, uncapped his pen, marked an item. He handed the newspaper to Empton. Empton snatched it. He read the item. He stared at Gently.

'So?' he said softly.

'So we're ready to charge him,' Gently said. 'Just as soon as we can pick him up. I'm afraid you're wasting your time, old man.'

Empton dropped the newspaper on the desk, walked round
the desk, sat down on the edge of it. He took out his cigarette-
case, took from it a yellow cigarette, looked at the cigarette
for a moment, rolled it between his lips, flicked a light
for it, sucked. He looked at the angle of the wall and the
ceiling.

'I see,' he said. 'Men at work.'

He sucked in air along with the smoke and forced the smoke
through his nostrils.

'And you've got it all tied up,' he said. 'Ready to hit me
over the head with it. You ring for Joe to open the tin, then
shunt him off back to stores.' He sucked hard. 'Congratula-
tions. Nice timing and all that. Trusting I gave every satisfac-
tion, must hurry away to other clients.'

'Jan,' Gently said. 'You can go.'

'Yes, you can go, Jan,' Empton said. 'We'll give you a ring
if your alibi's faked. Slide. Shove off. Blow. Fade.'

'Unless Superintendent Empton has any questions,' Gently
said.

'Oh, laughable,' Empton said. 'Run along Jan. Sling your
hook, Jan. Love and kisses to Mr. Razek.'

Kasimir rose, hesitated. 'I will answer the questions,' he
said.

'Dear boy,' Empton said. 'Remind me to send you a card
at Christmas.'

Kasimir gave his little shrug, picked up his possessions from
the desk. His lips were puffed, his face bruised. He held his
back very stiffly. To Gently he said:

'I have Flat 5A, 22 Bonser Street, West Hampstead. My

alibi is not a fake. You will find me there if you want me again.'

'Leave me your handkerchief,' Empton said.

Kasimir bowed. He went out.

Nobody said anything for a little while. Empton sucked and exhaled noisily. Whitaker fiddled with a pen-stand on the desk. Gently sat and did nothing. At last Empton ground out the cigarette.

'Right,' he said. 'So I'm a bastard.' He turned about to look at the two of them. 'But I'm a good bastard, in my line. It's a bastard line, let's face it. You don't kid-glove in M.I.5. And I'm a royal bastard in a nest of bastards. And that's my job. And the country pays me. So knock me down, point to the kennel. But remember who it was made Kasimir talk.'

Whitaker stirred. 'I don't know,' he said.

Empton's teeth showed. 'Why not, old man? Don't you know that Rule Britannia stinks outside the last night of the proms? We're a dirty lot at a dirty game, and so we pay dirty people like me. Sorry if the cloven hoof shows. We try to hide it from the taxpayer.'

'And you like your job?' Whitaker said.

Empton kept on smiling. 'I'm a natural bastard, old man,' he said. 'You can't do without me until the millennium.'

Whitaker dropped his eyes to the pen-stand, shook his head. 'I don't know,' he repeated.

'But you do, of course,' Empton said. 'Of course you do. Of course. Of course.'

'It's beyond me,' Whitaker said.

Empton chuckled. He looked pleased again.

He said to Gently: 'Can we get to business, and waste a little more of my time? It's faintly possible that there's still an angle which belongs to my department.'

'That's not improbable,' Gently said.

'You amaze me, old man,' Empton said.

Gently shrugged. 'Like you,' he said. 'I'd be interested to know who Teodowicz was.'

'Who he was?'

Gently nodded. 'It's just an idea that came into my head. And what links he had with Huxford. And the Poles who used to be there.'

Empton widened his eyes. 'Yes,' he said. 'This sounds amusing. Run over the details for me, old man. I may not be quite expended yet.'

Gently told him the details. Empton listened without questions. He sat on the desk looking straight at Gently, quite still, never moving his head. Gently looked at him occasionally. Empton's stare never shifted. Whitaker had pulled a little aside, was twiddling his fingers, frowning at them. Gently finished.

'Yes . . . I see,' Empton said. 'It fits together like a Swiss watch. Mysterious calls, the missing gun, the van parked by a main-line station. But don't you think it stinks a little, old man?'

'I'm open to reactions,' Gently said.

'My name is mud,' Empton said, 'but I can't help twigging a faint aroma. You look for the gun. You go to the nearest aerodrome. Immediately everything is falling into place. Your chummie is pin-pointed, motive, opportunity, nothing is left to the imagination. Oh, I'm a Special Branch man, I see a bogey in every bush. But in my doubtful opinion there is a definite pong.'

'Well,' Gently said.

'A pong of contrivance,' Empton said. 'The sort of contrivance one might expect from some thorough-going professionals. The sort of people with devious minds who like to tuck in the loose ends, who take a pride in their craft. People like me, in fact.' The teeth appeared. 'Another small point. Weren't you surprised by Kasimir's ineptness? How easy it was for you to spot him, and how excruciatingly innocent he was? He was bloody amateurish, old man, he was staked out for our inspection. We're supposed to think that Razek knows nothing and is quite upset about poor Teodowicz. Meanwhile, lo and behold! a chummie. A chummie framed up to his eyeballs.'

'It could be,' Gently said.

'A pity I've lost my credit,' Empton said.

Gently was silent, then he said: 'In your opinion, what was behind it?'

'Half a compliment,' Empton said. 'I think Teodowicz was important. I've held that opinion all along. He was some kind of a big wheel.'

'What sort of a big wheel?'

'Perhaps an organizer,' Empton said. 'A man who directed other agents and acted as a clearing-house for their reports. You noticed how his documents were destroyed? That would scarcely have happened to mere account-sheets. But there could have been other stuff amongst them, perhaps micro-printed or in code. And remember his freedom to travel about. I think he was a man in Razek's position.'

'Then why would they kill him?'

'Simple, old man. They found they couldn't trust him any longer. If he were only an agent they could have shopped him or used him for dropping duff info, but there's only one way with a big wheel. He knows too much. You have to kill him. And when you kill him,' Empton said, 'you have to kill his smell along with him. So you lay on a scapegoat, like this Sawney, and expend a pawn, like little Jan. There's the pattern. It adds up nicely. Razek is one of their top men.'

'Hmn,' Gently said. 'It skips a few factors.'

Empton's teeth showed. 'Naturally, old man. I don't have the acumen of a homicide brass, I have to lean on my pitiful experience. Have you an alternative view to air?'

Gently shook his head. 'I'll agree with you so far. There's something too slick about the case against Sawney, though I don't have my finger on it yet.'

'But nothing political. Of course.'

'I don't,' Gently said, 'rule it out. But there is nothing pointing that way at the moment. Except the way one interprets the facts.'

Empton laughed, rose from the desk. 'So bracing,' he said, 'these departmental conferences. But I think I'll follow my own ideas, crude and fantastic though they are. I'm going to poach in your covert, old man, I'm going to have a snout round Huxford. There may be some evidence gone begging there which only a fanatic like me would appreciate. You've no objection I suppose, old man?'

'None, old man,' Gently said.

'English justice,' Empton said. He crossed to the door, went out.

Whitaker pushed the pen-stand away from him, sprawled a little in his chair. He stuck clasped hands under his chin, looked at the closed door vacantly. He shook his head once.

'Extraordinary type. Extraordinary,' he said.

Gently shrugged.

'No, but really,' Whitaker said. 'Do they have many like him in Whitehall?'

*　　　*　　　*

Afternoon, Friday August 16th. Dust hanging in the tired hedges. The hot breath of heavy vehicles tossing the paper rubbish along the verge. The sun high, molten, stingy. The sky hard except at the edges. Mirages winking in the hollows of the road. Air shimmering over the dark tarmac. Tiny wind-devils, whirling straws and dust, springing up suddenly in the parched fields. The towers of Bintly, marching, marching. The air dead, the air pressing. Tyres wearing on the

133

greasy road. More tyres. More tyres. Northing and southing along the earth. As she dances about the sun.

Gently came to The Raven.

The notice on the door said CLOSED and the curtains in the parlour windows were drawn. No sound came from the building. The park was empty of vehicles. He slammed the door of the 105, went over, knocked, stood listening. The knock had a slight echo. No sound followed the knock. He walked a few paces from the door, peered into one of the un-curtained windows; walked to the end of the long stroke, stared round it into the yard, the unkempt garden. A black-and-white kitten lay asleep in the garden. The kitten woke up, ran across to him, purred. He tickled the kitten behind the ears. The kitten left him. He returned to the park. As he turned the corner a curtain moved and he went straight to the door and knocked again. This time he heard soft move-ments. The door was unbolted and opened by Wanda. She was wearing a green raincoat which she was holding closed. She looked at him. She had no expression.

'You want to come in?' she said.

'Yes,' Gently said. 'I hope it's convenient.'

'I haven't got a man here', Wanda said, 'if that's what you mean, and I presume it is. I was lying down, you woke me up. You can come in, I don't care.'

She stood back. Gently entered. She closed and bolted the door again. She stopped holding the rain-coat closed. It fell open. She was naked under it.

'Well?' she said.

'I'll just look through the place.'

He walked swiftly through the kitchen, through the toilets, to the back door. It was bolted. He opened it. The garden, the field showed empty. The kitten had gone back to sleep again, didn't cock its head at the sound of the door. He closed and re-bolted it. He returned quickly to the front door.

134

He lifted the curtain and looked out. The 105 stood quietly shimmering.

'Satisfied?' Wanda said. 'If I had a bloke here I'd show him. I'd like to think you were jealous, of course, only you don't seem the jealous type.'

He said nothing. He went into the parlour, through the parlour into her bedroom. The bed was dishevelled as though it had been lain on. There was a smell of cigarette-smoke. He came out, went to the guest-lounge, the toilets, the range of twelve bedrooms. Under its tin roof the building was oven-hot and sweat was glistening on his face. He returned to the parlour. Wanda had discarded the rain-coat. She lay on the studio couch, smoking a cigarette. She too had a shine on her forehead and on her body a film of perspiration. One knee was crooked, a hand trailing. She blew smoke upwards. Her eyes followed the smoke.

'Am I bothering you?' she asked. 'I don't think I am, but I could be wrong. This is my own house and it's a warm day, you have to take me as you find me.'

Gently shook his head. 'You don't bother me.'

'Perhaps you'd rather I was dressed,' Wanda said. 'Perhaps you'd like me in fur or with black suspenders. I don't mind. I have a wide repertoire.'

'I'm sure you have,' Gently said.

'Yes, I have,' Wanda said. 'Don't waste your talent for sarcasm, I know my business, I take a pride in it. Every man is a little different, wants a special twist to make him happy. I like to find out the twist. I'm quite a psychologist in my way.'

'Who is it smokes in your bedroom?' Gently said.

'I smoke in my bedroom,' Wanda said. 'Do you find it inhibiting, or something. That's a new one on me.'

'I just find it interesting,' Gently said. 'There weren't any ends in the ash-tray. And you haven't any stain on your finger. I don't think you smoke them much, do you?'

'Do you want a fag?' Wanda said.

'No,' Gently said. 'I smoke a pipe.'

'Of course,' Wanda said. 'I like pipe-smokers. A man with a pipe always attracts me.' She fanned some smoke. 'There was one bloke I knew who always wanted the radio on. Not in the bedroom, but out here. Did you ever know of a bloke like that? Then there was Pete, he was Irish, it took me a long time to figure him. He liked me to blindfold him with a stocking, but I had to find out, he wouldn't tell me. Men. There's no two alike. I could have told Havelock Ellis some new ones. I'm not boring you, by any chance?'

'You're not boring me,' Gently said.

'I get carried away,' Wanda said. 'It's one of the subjects I never tire of. And men like to talk about it, as a rule, it helps them to shed their inhibitions.' She sat up, swung her feet to the floor. 'I'm going into the bedroom,' she said.

'Why?' Gently said.

She shrugged her lean shoulders. 'Who knows?' she said. 'I was never a quitter.'

She rose, went through into the bedroom. Gently hesitated, followed after her. The square bedroom window was closed and curtained and the curtain was yellow and made the room yellowish. She gave a few more puffs to her cigarette and then stubbed it in the tray. She went to the wardrobe and opened the door, stood looking at the clothes inside.

'Are you sure I shouldn't dress a little?' she said. 'I could bear a girdle, something of that sort.'

'It would be a waste of time,' Gently said.

'I've some mink garters.'

He didn't say anything. He walked across to the inside wall, tapped it, put his shoulder against it. The wall was made of panelled hardboard. He ran his fingers over it. They came away dusty.

'Positively no deception,' Wanda said. 'That backs on the lounge if you want to know. There's a three-inch air space between the panels, that's all. No concealed doors.'

'Thank you for the information,' Gently said.

'Oh, no charge,' Wanda said. 'But I wish you wouldn't be so damned professional, even here, in my very bedroom.'

'I'm here professionally,' Gently said.

'We could still be friends,' she said, 'while you're about it. As I said before, I'm not trying to bribe you, you're welcome to prowl and ask what you like.'

'Do you take a paper?' Gently asked.

'Not *The Times*. But I take one.'

'We have a case against Sawney,' Gently said. 'If we want to press that case, of course.'

She looked at him. Her eyes were narrowed. 'Is that supposed to mean something?' she said. 'I couldn't care less what happened to Sawney, your beautiful subtlety is being wasted.'

'It means we're not certain that Sawney did it. Though the evidence is stacked against him.'

'Hurrah for Sawney,' Wanda said. 'It'll make a nice surprise for him when you catch him. Who is the leading suspect now?'

'Perhaps somebody not very far away.'

'How exciting,' Wanda said. 'No wonder I don't seem able to hold your attention.'

She closed the door of the wardrobe, came over, stood close beside him.

'Can't you forget it for just a moment,' she said. 'We can always talk about it some other time.' She brushed against him, stood firm. 'It's so damned hot,' she said. 'You look boiled in all those clothes. I shan't pinch your wallet. Take them off. I'm not boring you?'

Gently shrugged. She moved away from him, sat on the

bed. Her shiny face looked up at him. The eyes were smiling. The lips didn't smile.

'You remind me of a kid I had here once,' she said. 'He was another queer customer. He'd never made any love before. He was stark scared to take his clothes off.'

Gently took the chair and sat on it. She watched him, the eyes still smiling.

'And Tom,' she said. 'There was Tom. He liked me to tie him up with lighting flex. Hand and foot.' She patted the bed-frame. 'Then he struggled and groaned all the time. You know about that sort of thing, do you? I should think the police know a good deal about it.'

'It isn't my department,' Gently said. 'I'm a homicide specialist.'

'It's wrong to specialize too much,' she said. 'You could be extending your general knowledge. I'm a specialist too, in my way, and my subject isn't quite so morbid.'

He didn't say anything, sat quite still, listened to the heavy silence of the building; the silence existing outside the moan of the traffic, which sounded subdued. In the room it was very silent. He could hear the quickness of Wanda's breathing. Her eyes were narrowing as the pause lengthened. At last she moved, making the springs creak.

'So I'm a specialist,' she went on. 'And this is my laboratory, in here. That's why it's a bare little room and why it's a bare little bed. I want to control all the stimuli when I'm engaged in an experiment, I want to know exactly how they tick. I ought to keep bloody records. What are you thinking about?'

'Hmn,' Gently said. 'I was thinking how quiet it was.'

'It's always quiet,' Wanda said. 'You don't hear the traffic after a while. You don't want the radio on, do you?'

'No,' Gently said.

'Thank heaven for that. One of that type is enough, I don't want to be stuck with another one.'

138

She leaned forward, elbows on knees, chin rested on her hands, bringing her face to front his, easing forward to the edge of the bed.

'Are you married?' she said.

He shook his head.

'Got a woman?'

He shook it again.

'You like me,' she said. 'You think I'm a nympho, but you like me. And I am a nympho. I admit that. I've got the appetite of the devil. I had a man when I was twelve and I was playing around before that. But that's all. That's saying it all. That's just the way I happen to be. I may be a liar into the bargain, but that's something you can't help. I'm nothing else, and you know it. And you like me. Though you won't play.'

'Where are you going?' Gently said.

The eyes didn't smile. 'I'm not going anywhere.'

'You're going somewhere,' Gently said. 'What's the end going to be?'

'Don't get moral,' Wanda said. 'My father was a moralist. I've heard too much of it. And he finished up in court over a schoolboy, but he was as moral as they come.'

'I wasn't being moral,' Gently said. 'A policeman sees too much to be moral. I was being practical. You're planning to leave here. I was asking what the end was to be.'

She breathed harder, looking at him. He could smell the sharpness of her perspiration.

*　　　*　　　*

'Who says I was planning to leave here?' Her husky voice had a rougher edge on it. Her eyes were wide, challenging, the pupils enlarged by the dim light.

'Nobody said it,' Gently said. 'It's merely a logical deduction. When the heat is slackened a little you'll be off. When you think it's safe to make a move.'

'What are you saying?' she said. 'I'm free to come and go as I please. I don't know what the devil you think you've got on me, but it isn't true, whatever it is. You can't touch me.'

Gently nodded. 'We can limit your movements.'

'Like hell you can,' Wanda said.

'Yes,' Gently said, 'and we can cordon this place. That will mean nobody coming in, going out, except we check their credentials, and your phone tapped too. And a tail on you. Think what that's going to mean.'

'You bloody bastard,' Wanda said. 'You think I'll lie down under police persecution? I'll get a lawyer, I'll talk to the press. I'll tell them you've laid me from here to breakfast.'

'But what's the end going to be?' Gently said. 'Do you even know the next step? You're right. I like you. I don't think you're dirt. But you'll be over the edge if you run from here.'

She dragged back from him, pulling on her knees. 'I go where I like, screw,' she said. 'I don't ask anyone what I do, and I don't want to hear anyone telling me. I've had a lot of that from people, from my father, my husband, divorce-court judges—men, the whole bloody bag of them! Filthy bastards. Filthy men. Men who invented bloody morals so they could sneer at women they couldn't get—that's the long and the short of morals. Have you ever thought about it, screw?'

Gently shrugged. 'You could be right—'

'Too true I'm right,' she interrupted. 'I'm not dumb. I don't just take it. I can see through their dirty tricks. If I believed them I'd hang myself for being outside the pale—some bloody sub-creature who shouldn't breathe. That's what I'd do with myself. But it's a lie. A stinking lie. And I'll ram it back down their throats. To hear a man talk of morals is enough to make an angel puke.'

'I'm not talking of morals,' Gently said.

'You sounded like it,' Wanda said. 'And I'm just warning you not to do it, I've had all I can take of that sort of thing. Always I've had it, right from the start. From men as randy as old toms. You lock your bedroom door on a man and he begins to be moral. You know', she said, 'what I think of men? I think of men as bits of stuff. That's what, bits of stuff. That's how men rate with me.'

'That's your privilege,' Gently said.

'Bits of stuff,' Wanda said. 'Here and there a decent one, but the rest, bits of stuff.'

Gently said: 'And because of that you refuse your dues to society.'

'What dues,' Wanda said. 'Society stinks and you know it. Top to bottom it's all this.' She made a grasping gesture with her hand. 'A fat lot of dues I owe society and its paid thugs, like you.'

'You have protection from it,' Gently said. 'The least you can do is pay it back.'

'I don't owe it anything,' Wanda said. 'It isn't me who's in the red.'

'A man was killed. You might be killed. His killer is loose. So might be your killer. That isn't morality, it's the main chance. You want to stop alive, don't you?'

'Why should he kill me?' Wanda said.

'Because you know too much,' Gently said. 'And you're very vulnerable although you're so useful. I don't think you're intended to leave this place.'

'You shut up,' Wanda hissed. 'I don't like that kind of talk.'

'You're not intended to leave,' Gently said, 'because you're a liability as well as a threat. One can disappear more easily than two, especially when the other one is a woman. Look at it straight. Society stinks. Why are you hoping to be the exception?'

'Just button your mouth up, you bloody screw!'

'Why?' Gently said. 'Can somebody hear us?'

'I told you,' she hissed. 'I don't like that kind of talk. It isn't so clever, scaring a woman.'

'You went in with your eyes open,' Gently said. 'You don't have any illusions when it comes to men. So I'm not telling you anything you don't know, you must be conscious of where you stand.'

She jumped up off the bed. 'And you,' she said. 'Are you never scared? When you know such a bloody sight more than is good for you—aren't you scared of winding up in a ditch?'

He shrugged. 'It wouldn't be wise to kill me. I'm part of a large organization. But you're alone. That's your boast. You don't wear society's clothes.'

'Get out of here,' Wanda said. 'I'm tired of listening to you, screw. You don't kid me, I'm not playing your game, just take yourself out of my house.'

'You know where you stand,' Gently said.

'Yes,' she said. 'I know that. And society and the lot can go to hell. And you too. I'm not playing.'

Gently shook his head. 'You're not a cynic, you're a romantic,' he said. He got up. 'The second one I've had to do with today.'

'Clever, no doubt,' Wanda said. 'Next time remember to bring a warrant.'

'I hope I'll need it,' Gently said. 'This is a very quiet place.'

She flung out of the bedroom. He stood listening. Only the pad of her bare feet. He went after her. She'd got the door open. He paused on the threshold. She eyed him angrily.

'Put some clothes on,' he said. 'You know I'm not trying to kid you.'

'Play the tune somewhere else,' she said. 'This is the way I like to be.'

'Men don't always fall on the bed.'

142

Some are bloody eunuchs,' she said.

'Not when the hangman is round the corner.'

'Go to hell,' Wanda said. 'Ponce.'

He went out. She slammed the door. He heard the bolt shot, the brush of her feet. The noise of the traffic was suddenly loud, dulling the sensitivity of his ears. He went slowly to the 105, unlocked it, got in, left the door open. The heat inside made his skin prickle and brought out a fresh lacing of sweat. He sat with one leg out of the door. He took his pipe from the stowage, filled and lit it. The traffic kept rolling by, self-intent, pounding trucks, impatient cars. Few of the drivers looked at The Raven. The Raven stood by itself. Tired timber, rusting red roof, untidy park, derelict pumps. By itself under the sun. A few yards away from the Road's thunder. The windows blind with faded curtains, the notice on the door saying CLOSED. Gently smoked, wiped his face. None of the curtains showed movement. No sound came from the building that could be heard above the traffic. He went on smoking till the tobacco was burned out. Still the silence beside clamour. He knocked out the pipe on his palm, closed the door, pressed the starter.

Going northwards was a Commer truck squarely loaded with wooden crates. The truck was overtaken by two cars, then by the 105, touching the sixties. The sound of the truck vanished behind. About ten seconds later came another sound. It was a persistent rattle which seemed to shake the car and which ended in the shattering of the rear offside-door window. Along with this rattle was a background noise. It sounded like a very fast pneumatic drill. The 105 swerved. There was a thudding patter behind it. Gently went on driving fast, pulled in half a mile down the road. In the driving mirror he saw the Commer following him. It slowed, braked. A man got down.

The man came running round to the 105, a hard-framed man with a sunken-cheeked face. He grabbed the door and hauled it open, stared at Gently with white-rimmed eyes.

'Blimey!' he said. 'Are you all right, cock?'

Gently said nothing, got out of the car.

'You were bloody strafed, cock!' the man gabbled. 'Christ, what's it coming to on this sodding road?'

'Did you cop any?' Gently said.

'Not for want of him trying,' the man said. 'He was in the bushes. Up at the lay-by. I was shitting myself, I daren't stop.'

'Did you get a look at him?'

'Not bloody likely. Just the smoke, I could see that.'

'Get back in your truck,' Gently said. 'Drive to Everham phone-box. Inform the Offingham police.'

The man stared, his mouth open. 'What are you going to do, cock?' he said.

'Police,' Gently said. 'I've got a job here. Get back in your truck and warn Offingham.'

He walked round the car. The nearside panels were perforated in a line that slanted upwards. The line began at the bottom of the front door and wavered uncertainly to the smashed rear door window. At the back of the car was a scattered group of deep dents, but no penetration. None of the tyres had been punctured. Only the one window was broken.

'Blimey!' the man said, coming to look. 'You're a lucky bastard, you are. If he'd held that frigger straight you wouldn't be worrying about the bomb.'

'Go and get that call made,' Gently said.

'You're going after him?' the man said.

'Just do what I ask you,' Gently said.

The man looked at him, frowning. He shook his head. 'You're mad,' he said. 'But I'm a mad bugger too, I was in the Parachute Regiment. It'll need a couple of us, I reckon, if we're going to stand a chance. You lay for him, I'll draw him. I've got a wrench in the truck you can have.'

Gently said: 'You'll get in that truck and you'll drive straight to Everham phone-box. You'll ring the Offingham police and you'll tell them that a wanted man is in the vicinity of The Raven roadhouse. Tell them that the message is from Superintendent Gently and that he wants road blocks and a cordon round the area. Tell them that the man is armed with a Sten gun and that revolvers are to be issued. Have you got all that?'

The man swallowed. 'I've got it,' he said.

'Do it directly,' Gently said. 'I may be prevented from getting to a telephone. What's your name?'

'Sam Ives. I come from Harlow New Town.'

'On your way,' Gently said.

Ives went back to the Commer, jumped in.

Gently got in the 105, backed it on the verge, swung it round. He drove slowly towards the lay-by. He watched the traffic coming north. There was a big articulated coming north with other traffic hung behind it. He put on speed. He passed the lay-by almost square with the articulated. He kept accelerating. He didn't hear anything. He braked by The Raven, cut across to it, parked. He went to the door and wrenched at the handle, drove his foot into it. The door fell open. Wanda came running from the kitchen. She was dressed. She carried a handbag.

'You!' Wanda said. Her eyes were fearful. 'You aren't hurt—he didn't hurt you?'

Gently brushed past her. He grabbed the phone, began to spin off a number.

'You bloody fool,' Wanda screamed. 'He's coming back. He's going to kill you. Get to hell out of this place, you can't stop in here.'

'You can't stop here either,' Gently said. 'Take the car. Drive to Baddesley.'

'Oh God Oh God,' she cried. 'He's going to kill you, he's going to kill you.'

'Take the car,' Gently said. 'Police. Superintendent Gently speaking.'

'Oh God,' Wanda sobbed. Her stub heels pattered out through the kitchen. The car door slammed, the engine started. The car didn't pull away.

'You've had a message from Ives,' Gently said. 'If you haven't, this is the message.'

He held the receiver away from his ear, listening, watching, his back to the wall. He spoke softly.

'Right. You're getting it. I'm at The Raven. He's somewhere close. Come straight to The Raven. Put a cordon round it. Take special care to cover the fields. Set up road blocks at Everham and Huxford to stop all traffic. Send them armed.'

He stopped speaking. The black-and-white kitten had run in from outside. It ran up to Gently, rubbed against his ankle, purred, whisked its tail, stalked away. He hung up the receiver very quietly, began to move along the corridor. He could hear nothing except the 105's engine filling in the gaps in the traffic.

He came to the toilets, listened, slid into them, came to the back door. It was unbolted. The kitten was following him. It went to the door and looked up at it. He moved across to the door, listened again, eased the bolts home. The kitten still looked at the door. There was no sound from outside it. He moved back into the corridor, looked along the doors of the bedrooms. They were closed. He returned to the kitchen. The café was empty. The parlour was empty. The kitten ran ahead into the narrow room, stopped, looked back at Gently. It didn't look about the narrow room. Gently went in. The kitten proceeded. It entered the bedroom, stood switching its tail. Gently approached the door of the bedroom. He looked into the bedroom.

The bedroom was not as he had last seen it. The bed had been moved to one side. The lino from under the bed was rolled up and a section of the floor-boards had been lifted. There was a cavity below the floor-boards which was about four feet deep. Its walls were supported by rough timber baulks and the floor was covered with dirty floor-cloth. On the floor-cloth stood a camp-bed and on the bed lay an electric lantern, and beside the bed was a jug of lemonade and a glass and a stuffed ash-tray. A section of six-inch drain pipe projected from one of the walls and a faint light showed in it. The removed floor-boards lay on Wanda's bed. They were a section which matched the existing cross-fit of the floor.

He didn't go into the room but stood looking. The kitten moved around, sniffed at the cavity. The yellow curtains of the square window were drawn back. The window was part open. There was a faint draught from it. Then the window darkened a little and Gently looked at the window. The face of a man was squinting through it. Their eyes met. The man was a stranger. He began to fire through the wall as Gently leaped backwards. The gun kept firing, raking splinters off the door-frame. Gently wasn't hit. He ran back into the parlour. Wanda was screaming 'This way, this way.' He ran out into the park. The gun had stopped firing. Wanda had the 105's door open. She was screaming. He jumped into the car. She crashed home the clutch, bucked the car away.

'Not too far!' Gently shouted at her. 'The gun doesn't have any range.'

'He'll kill the pair of us. He'll kill us.'

'Don't go further than the bend!'

She was driving madly, her foot down, swerving the 105 dangerously. He reached for the key, turned it, withdrew it. The car slowed, came to a rest, finished partly on the verge. She was sobbing and screaming. 'No—no!' He slapped her face. It had no effect. 'He'll kill us—he will—he'll kill us, he'll kill us!' 'Shut up,' Gently said. 'He's still back there behind the building.' She tried to open the door. He knocked her hands away from it. She screamed piercingly in her fear.

'Who is it?' Gently said. His eyes were hard on the building, isolating it. Nobody had come round either end of it, or through the door, still sagging open.

'He won't stop at you. He'll kill both of us.'

'What's his name—who is he?'

'Oh God let's go, let's go.'

'Tell me who he is,' Gently said.

She struggled again. He pinned her down. She tried to strike him. She was too weak. She sobbed and cried in frantic panic, making efforts to get the door handle. The moments passed, became minutes. Still nobody came round the building. The kitten appeared for a moment at the door, turned round deliberately, marched in again. Wanda's struggles became less continuous. Her sobs declined into a moaning.

'He's a Pole, isn't he?' Gently said.

She whined. She went for the handle again.

'Is he someone who was here during the war—one of the Poles who were at Huxford?'

'Find out, you bugger,' she whined.

'How long has he been hiding at The Raven?'

'Find out,' she said. 'Find out. I tried to stop him going after you.'

'How were you going to get away?'

'I don't know,' she said. 'I don't know.'

'Because you weren't going to leave with him,' Gently said. 'He's a psychopath. He'd kill anyone.'

She moaned, struck at him. Her eyes hated him.

'You too,' Gently said. 'You'd like me to think that you're man-proof. But he got round you. And he's a killer.'

'He'll kill you,' Wanda said.

'Is he your husband?' Gently asked.

She tugged savagely. 'Talk bloody sense.'

'We'll find out,' Gently said. 'He's shot his bolt.'

Two minutes. Three minutes. Wanda was quiet but breathing heavily. There was a big gap in the traffic coming along, the north-bound traffic: the block was operating. The south-bound traffic continued to flow. Nothing moved up at The Raven. The door was hanging on one of its hinges, caved inwards, hanging still. Gently looked steadily at Wanda. He put the key back in the switch.

'I'm going back there,' he said. 'If he comes this way, don't wait for him.'

'No!' she cried. 'You can't do that. He won't give in, he'd sooner shoot you.'

'I'm not relying on it,' Gently said. 'Don't take the car except to avoid him. The road is blocked in both directions. Wait here. Unless he comes.'

'No.' She clung to him. 'Don't go after him. You can't do anything. He's got the gun.'

'Yes,' Gently said. 'He's got the gun.' He pulled loose from her, got out of the car.

There was a gate in the hedge, into the field. He went to the gate and looked through it. The field was a small field of turnips and had a cross-hedge near to the gate. He climbed the gate, approached the cross-hedge, found a gap through which to spy. Through the gap he could see The Raven at about a hundred yards distance. The garden was fenced with wire-netting. He could see most of the garden. At the end of the garden were the fruit trees and from it a hedge extended to the hedge he stood by. He worked up the field to the line of this hedge. It bounded also the field of turnips. He passed through it near a small field oak, proceeded along it till he came to the garden. He looked up the garden. He saw the yard. He saw where the man had stood when he was shooting. A scatter of shells lay about the spot, a few splinters of pinkish wood. Nothing moved. Between the yard and the fruit trees stood a poultry house with a sagged roof. He crept through the hedge, through the trees, came to the poultry house, stopped to observe. Nothing again. He moved rapidly into the yard, tried the door. It was still bolted.

He spent ten seconds listening, then came out of the yard and went to the bedroom window. Beneath it was chewed a savage rent through the wall timber and the hardboard lining. The rent was about the size of a dinner plate. He looked through it. He saw the kitten. The kitten was by the door and stretching its neck to sniff at a scar in the door frame. The room had no other occupant and the only sound was made by the kitten. He looked through the window into the cavity. There was nobody in the cavity. He looked along the wall towards the road, along the strip of ground between the wall and the fence. It was a part of the property not often trodden and was dripped on from the eaves and had a sandy surface. He trod on the surface. It gave a print. There were no other prints towards the road. He moved along it very quietly, came to the end of the short stroke where the gable faced the road. He looked up the road. Wanda was staring at him. There was now no traffic on the road. He picked up a stone, smashed the parlour window, ran quickly into the park, stood listening near the door. No sound. No movement. The kitten ran to meet him. He bent to stroke the kitten. He went in through the door.

Empty. Silent. The man had never entered the building.

Gently checked through it quickly, no longer cautious. Since the shooting ten or twelve minutes had passed. The man had retreated through the fields after the shooting. The man wasn't obsessed by his intention to kill Gently. The man was acting intelligently to retrieve his rashness. His retreat had perhaps taken him clear of the cordon which would be a local one concentrated on The Raven. Gently went to the phone, dialled, waited.

'Superintendent Gently. Is the cordon in position?'

'Yes sir,' the station sergeant replied. 'They should've set it up by now, sir.'

'Are you in contact?'

'Yes sir.'

'I want the cordon set wider. The chummie has taken off from The Raven and is somewhere in the area north of it. He's been gone over ten minutes. I want a cordon with a radius of two miles.'

'Yes sir. I've got that, sir. But I don't know if we've got the men, sir.'

'Get on to the next county. We're after a killer. Contact the army if that'll be quicker.'

He put down the phone, turning suddenly. A man was standing in the kitchen doorway. The man had a gun pointed at Gently. The man was Felling. His eyes were squinting.

'All right,' Gently snapped. 'Drop the gun. Our man has gone.'

Felling swayed a little. He was trembling. Then he relaxed. He lowered the gun.

*　　　*　　　*

Whitaker came in with Rice and Freeman. The two detective constables were carrying guns.

'We've just caught your message on the radio,' Whitaker said. 'What's been going on out here?'

Gently hunched. 'It's the way you heard it. The chummie has legged it across the fields. He came out of his hole to take a pot at me and I managed to get between him and the hole. He did some more shooting and I had to draw off. He didn't wait. That's the story.'

'Who is it—Sawney? Whitaker asked.

'No, not Sawney,' Gently said.

'Not Sawney?'

Gently shook his head. 'A stranger. A Pole, I think he is.'

'Did you get a look at him?'

'In a sort of way.' Gently's eyebrows lifted, slanted. 'He showed his face at a window for a moment, then he started shooting. I had to leave.'

'So what's he like?' Whitaker said.

'About fifty, tallish,' Gently said. 'High cheek-bones, big chin, mid-brown hair, flattish nose, eyes paleish, deep lines. He can use a Sten but he isn't an expert.'

'He was using a Sten?'

'He was using a Sten.'

'You've got a guardian angel,' Whitaker said. 'I'd still have been running if he'd fired at me. Even one bullet makes me nervous. But this is a turn-up,' he said. 'If he isn't Sawney, who the devil is he?'

'Mrs. Lane knows,' Gently said. 'But Mrs. Lane isn't telling.'

'And he was hiding here?'

'Under her bedroom. And the hideout wasn't thought up in a hurry. I think there was a good deal of planning in this, I think it dates back further than Saturday.'

'Hah,' Whitaker said. 'Sounds like Empton.'

'No,' Gently said. 'Non-political. This is the crime of an individual. A crime of revenge. But not Sawney's. Perhaps if we get those Polish records from Huxford we'll be able to spot what's happened. Or maybe it's a job for Interpol, perhaps they can tell us more about Teodowicz.'

'Or perhaps chummie will talk,' Whitaker said. 'He won't get far. I've got the dogs coming.'

'He's got the gun,' Gently said.

'Yes,' Whitaker said. 'But he's one man.'

*　　　*　　　*

The dogs arrived in a van. Two Alsatians with bloody eyes. They yelped and whined and heaved on their leads as they dragged their handlers into Wanda's bedroom. Wanda was sitting in the parlour under the supervision of Rice. Her small mouth was very small, she didn't have any smile in her eyes. The dogs yelped around the cavity. Freeman got in, handed up the mattress. The dogs fell on the mattress, tread on it, snuffing it, dragging out the smell of the man who had the gun. Their tails swept busily, they quivered, trembled. Their black muzzles poked everywhere. They stood off, gave voice.

One of the handlers said: 'Where shall we start them, sir?'

'Bring them round to the back,' Gently said.

The dogs were brought there. They whined and snuffled, followed trails and cross-trails in and out of the yard. Then one of them lifted its wedge-shaped head and bayed wolf-like from the depth of its throat. It started forward: it went straight down the garden. The second dog yelped and struggled after it. Beyond the gap they were baffled temporarily, but then picked up the fresher scent and pointed out over the field. Gently, Whitaker, Felling followed after the handlers. Freeman came last, wearing a walkie-talkie set. The field was a stubble field about two hundred yards deep. The trail led towards a field gate beside which was a stile.

Whitaker said: 'These dogs will sort him out. I'd sooner have a dog than a gun any day. How far are we behind?'

'Half an hour,' Gently said.

'But there's the cordon,' Whitaker said. 'He's got to beat that, don't forget.'

Gently didn't say anything.

'Don't you think the cordon will hold him?' Whitaker said.

Gently hunched. 'This fellow is a planner.'

'But he didn't plan for this kind of thing,' Whitaker said. 'Not being hunted by dogs across open country. He couldn't have seen that coming off.'

'He was planning to leave somehow,' Gently said.

'No,' Whitaker said. 'We've busted his plan for him.'

Felling was walking along silently. He had his gun-holster unbuttoned.

They came to the field gate. The dogs barked at it. The gate was opened for them. They went ahead. Snuffling, gasping, heaving, whimpering, they dragged across a plot on which kale had been grown. Part of the kale crop was un-cut and stood on the right in a green reef. The trail passed close along the line of the standing kale, turned round the far side of it, entered a spinney of tall elms.

'Spread out here,' Whitaker ordered. 'We don't want to run into him in a bunch.'

The men spread out among the elms. They trampled the underbrush noisily. Felling stayed on the track hard behind the two handlers. The trail followed the track. The track had been rutted by cart wheels. It bore left, passed an empty cart-lodge, ran out of the trees, became a lane. In the lane a uniformed man was standing. He wore a gun. He had his hand on the gun.

'Anderson!' Whitaker bawled. 'Seen any signs of him yet?'

Anderson's hand went to his helmet. 'No sir,' he said. 'Haven't seen a soul, sir.'

'What are you doing this way, man?'

'I thought I'd close up, sir,' Anderson said. 'The army are

putting down a cordon behind us. Thought I'd close up towards The Raven.'

'Well, you can drop that idea, man,' Whitaker said. 'Tag along with the dogs, we can probably use you.'

They followed the lane. It ran between high hedges on which bunches of green berries had begun to redden. The dogs were never in any doubt, bullocked and snorted their way along it. Some distance ahead, beyond a screen of trees, one heard the occasional buzz of a vehicle. When he heard this noise Whitaker frowned. The noises became louder as they advanced.

'What road would that be?' Gently asked.

'The Bedford road,' Whitaker said.

'Does this lane join it?'

'Don't know,' Whitaker said. 'Would we join the road, Felling?'

'Yes sir,' Felling said. 'We join it. About four or five miles above Baddesley.'

Whitaker didn't comment, continued to frown, walked a little closer to the dogs.

They came up with the trees, which were a belt of poplars. They made on the left a small grove. An opening, flanked by old posts, gave access to the grove, and through the opening could be seen a hut. The hut was old and had felt peeling from its roof. It had double doors, not quite closed. Through the roof a rusty chimney projected and upturned over this was an empty tin. The printing on the tin was fresh printing. The dogs turned in here. They pointed to the hut.

'Hold them back!' Whitaker commanded. 'Nobody to approach that hut without orders. Felling, you take Freeman and Anderson, cover the hut from the rear.'

'Are we to shoot?' Felling said.

'If he bolts,' Whitaker said. 'But at the legs, Felling, at the legs. Unless he's blasting with the gun.'

Felling searched the hedge, found a gap to force, went through it followed by Freeman and Anderson. The dogs were hauling and struggling, but silent, their red eyes glowing at the hut. Whitaker turned to one of the handlers.

'Give your gun to the Superintendent. When Felling's set you're to take your dog up while the Super and I give you cover. I'll give the fellow a chance to come out. If he doesn't, pull a door open and let the dog in. Palmer, you'll let the other dog go. Keep on the ground, Jackson, when you get to the hut. You've got the idea?'

'Yes sir,' Jackson said.

'I'm putting you in because you're single,' Whitaker said. 'Sorry, man. It's a blasted job.'

'I don't mind, sir,' Jackson said.

Thirty seconds passed. They saw Felling. He was to the left of the hut, behind a tree. He looked at them, raised his hand warningly, looked behind the hut, kept it raised. Ten seconds later he lowered it.

'Right, Jackson,' Whitaker said.

Jackson went forward, his dog galloping, got to the hut, threw himself flat. Nothing stirred in the hut. Jackson had hold of the dog by its collar.

Whitaker shouted: 'You in there! We are the police, and we've got you surrounded. We are armed and we have dogs. I'm giving you ten seconds to come out. Come out with your hands above your head. I'm beginning to count now.'

Whitaker counted: One bloody second, two bloody seconds, up to ten. Nobody came out of the hut. Whitaker flashed his hand downwards. Jackson ripped open one of the doors, slipped the dog, rolled sideways. The dog crashed in through the door, snarling, clashing its white teeth. The other dog shot forward simultaneously. It went through the door. Both dogs were barking. Jackson scrambled up, ran into the hut. Palmer ran forward too. Whitaker ran. Gently walked.

'Oh, the bastard!' Whitaker said, staring.

The hut was empty except for two petrol cans. On the earthen floor were a number of oil stains and also the clear marks of car tyres. The dogs barked. They ran about excitedly. They wagged their tails. They whined at their handlers.

*   *   *

Gently said to Freeman: 'Get this message through directly. The wanted man has escaped in a car by way of the Bedford–Baddesley Road. Make and registration number unknown. The existing cordons to be called in. Set up road checks outside towns within a fifty mile radius and particularly on the London approaches. The man is armed and dangerous.'

'Roger, sir,' Freeman said, and began to speak into his microphone.

Whitaker was flushed, his eyes were angry. 'I'm a stupid so-and-so,' he said. 'You're right, this bloke isn't a rabbit, he'd got his escape route ready waiting. What else can we do?'

'We can try to find out the make and number of the car,' Gently said. 'The car has been garaged here for over a week. Somebody ought to know something about it.'

'Anderson!' Whitaker called, looking round. Anderson came up, still carrying his gun. 'Put that away,' Whitaker said. 'Anderson, who does this hut belong to?'

'It belongs to the farm, sir,' Anderson said. 'Holly Tree Farm, a Mr. Lemmon.'

'How far away?'

'About half a mile, sir.'

'We'll get over there,' Whitaker said. 'Palmer, Jackson, you take the dogs back. That was a nice piece of work, Jackson. Felling, you'd better come with us. And Freeman too, we may need the juke-box.'

They continued along the lane to its junction with the

157

Bedford–Baddesley road, turned right, followed the road to a second junction, beside which stood milk churns. A rutted drive led to a farmhouse with a straw thatched roof. A woman wearing an apron answered the door. They were shown into a kitchen where two men sat eating. The elder of the two rose.

'Hullo,' he said. 'Hullo.'

'Mr. Lemmon?' Whitaker said.

'Farmer Lemmon,' the man said. 'Joe Anderson here can tell you that.'

'We're trying to apprehend a man,' Whitaker said. 'We've tracked him into your hut in the poplar plantation. He appears to have had a car there. We'd like some information about that car.'

'About the car, eh?' Lemmon said. He was a broad-framed man with a thick-featured face. 'Well, I don't know a damn sight about that car. I never saw it. Did you, Phil?'

'No, I never saw it,' the younger man said. 'Been too busy cutting to nose around.'

'But I can tell you who owns it,' Lemmon said. 'And I reckon you can get your information from him. It's a foreign bloke what comes from Offingham—Madling, Madson, that's what his name is.'

'Ove Madsen?' Gently said.

'Ah, that'd be it,' Lemmon said. 'Comes from Offingham, runs a truck. He shifted some stuff for me at one time.'

'Madsen,' Whitaker said. 'Madsen. Madsen!'

'How long had the car been there?' Gently said.

'Last Saturday, wasn't it?' Lemmon said to Phil. 'Ah, last Saturday. He dropped by after tea. He'd bought this car, he said, and he hadn't space for it, would I mind him sticking it in the old hut. I said no, it wouldn't eat any grass, he could stick it there till he got rid of it. Come up here driving a green van . . . wait a minute. Wasn't he the partner of that bloke what got murdered?'

'Madsen,' Whitaker said. 'Can we use your phone, sir?'

'Help yourself,' Lemmon said. 'It's in the hall.'

'He'll be at the crematorium,' Felling said, looking at his watch. 'He got the funeral fixed up for four-thirty.'

'He'll be at the *what*?' Gently said, catching Felling's wrist.

'At the crematorium, sir.' Felling looked at Gently, looked away.

'You didn't tell me it was to be a cremation,' Gently said.

'The Westlow Chapel, sir,' Felling said. 'I didn't think to mention it was a crematorium.'

Gently released Felling's wrist, brushed by Whitaker into the hall. He picked up the phone book, flipped through it, picked up the phone, dialled.

'Westlow Chapel?' Gently said. 'Superintendent Gently, C.I.D. You have a cremation service in progress, subject Timoshenko Teodowicz. Stop the service immediately. The cremation must not proceed. If possible, detain the chief mourner, Ove Madsen. We'll have men out there directly.'

He broke the connection, dialled again.

'Superintendent Gently,' he said. 'I want a car sent out to Westlow Chapel to bring in Ove Madsen for questioning. Also make arrangements to collect the body of Teodowicz from Westlow Chapel. Yes . . . Teodowicz' body. Please attend to it directly.'

He broke the connection. Whitaker was staring at him.

'What the devil's all this about?' Whitaker said.

Gently shrugged, dialled again, hooked up a chair and sat down on it. Whitaker shook his big head, looked at Felling. Felling was silent.

'Superintendent Gently,' Gently said. 'Put me through to the stores, please.' He sat with his elbow on the hall table, his eyes dreamy, looking at nothing. Felling had shoved the kitchen door closed but through it came the drone of Lemmon's voice. There was also the clink of cutlery on plates and the sound of someone stirring his tea. 'Squadron-Leader Campling?' Gently said.

'Speaking,' Campling returned. 'I'm glad you've rung. We've got some results here you may find interesting. I've your Superintendent Empton with me, I think you'd better talk to him.'

'Is Brennan with you?' Gently asked.

'Yes,' Campling said. 'I'm handing you over.'

Empton came on. 'Hallo, old man,' Empton said. 'So glad I looked in here instead of going straight back to London. How is progress with you?'

'What have you got?' Gently said.

'A small item of detail,' Empton said. 'Something that required my frivolous knowledge. Those Polish records have come in. I've spent the afternoon going through them. I've also interrogated that little Welshman—Jones. You know the one I mean?'

'Yes, I know him,' Gently said.

'A remarkable memory he's got,' Empton said. 'Not always available to a straight question, but the stuff's there. If you put in a ferret.'

'So?' Gently said.

'So,' Empton said, 'I had him go through the records with me. He began to remember names and people, to recall little things that had gone on. Like a couple of Poles who'd been friends with Sawney, a sergeant-pilot and one of their policemen. Sawney was great buddies with these two. They used to prang the boozers together. And this fascinated me very much because of what the records said about them. They both came from the same town in Poland—the town of Grodz. Does it strike a chord?'

'Teodowicz came from there,' Gently said.

'I thought you might have forgotten,' Empton said. 'But you're so right, it's the same town, the three of them all came from Grodz. The sergeant-pilot was called Kielce—my pronunciation is authentic—and he was lost on a spy-dropping raid over Holland. The policeman returned to Poland after the war and went into the diplomatic service. At present he's on attachment in London. Isn't that a coincidence? Guess his name.'

'Would it be Razek?' Gently said.

'That's phenomenal,' Empton said. 'It could, it would be, and it is, my old friend Stephan Tadeusz Razek. Not just any Razek, you see. The full name is given here in the record. He came from Grodz. He was Sawney's buddie. And he sent little Jan to talk to Teodowicz.'

'Hmn,' Gently said. 'So what do you make of it?'

'What I've always made of it,' Empton said. 'In my crazy boy-scout way. I think it was Razek who ordered the killing. I'm not sure why, it might have been personal, both of them coming from the same town. But I'm sure he ordered it, just as I'm sure he set up his old buddie as the fall-guy. He knew the ropes here at Huxford, and he's not particularly a man of sentiment.'

'Has it occurred to you,' Gently said, 'that Sawney may have been the source of Razek's tip-off?'

'It has, old man,' Empton said. 'I do occasionally look all round my facts. But why should Sawney break up this racket by sticking Razek on to Teodowicz? The threat would have made Teodowicz toe the line, it didn't need to go any further. No, I think Sawney is innocent there. I think Razek got on to his man independently. What really stumps me is the reason for the killing, unless, as I said, the motive was personal. But that isn't terribly satisfying, old man. It may be for you, but it isn't for me.'

'It isn't for me either,' Gently said.

'Cheers,' Empton said. 'Perhaps you know the motive?'

'I don't know the motive,' Gently said. 'But I'm picking up someone who certainly does.'

Empton was silent, then he said: 'Not Madsen, surely?'

'Madsen for one,' Gently said. 'He knows. And I'm hoping I'll persuade him to talk very shortly. Would you care to come along to the station?'

'Charmed, old man,' Empton said. 'You may need me to help with the persuasion.'

'I'd like Campling and Brennan to come too,' Gently said. 'Would you mind handing me back to Campling?'

Campling came back. Gently said: 'I think you should be present at Offingham H.Q. We're dealing with some business that relates to Sawney and which will probably be helpful to you. And I'd like Brennan right away. I've got some jobs for him to do. Tell him to bring his outfit with him and Sawney's cards and a set of his dabs.'

'You want Brennan to do something for you?' Campling asked.

'Yes,' Gently said. 'I've a reason for asking.'

'Well, that's all right with me,' Campling said. 'I was just surprised that you wanted Brennan. We'll come right along.'

'Thank you,' Gently said. He rang off. He stood up. 'That's all,' he said. 'We can pick up Mrs. Lane on the way.'

Whitaker said: 'I'm not quite with you.'

'We'll have a meal,' Gently said. 'Then we'll talk.'

*   *   *

The early evening of Friday August 16th. Coloured shadows taking a slant in the market-place of Offingham. A man stripped to the waist sculling meditatively down the Ound. A man with a hose washing market refuse from the backs of the stalls, into a heap. Youths, girls, on the stroll. Cars parked near the pubs and cafés. Couples loitering on the towpath. Pensioners sitting with their pipes. Outside Police H.Q., a number of cars, some with pressmen sitting in them. A straight shaft of blue smoke from the fish-and-chip van by the conveniences. Windows open very wide. Doors open. Fans turning. A soundless chalkline extending itself across the deeper blue of the sky. In its brick tower, dusty, hot, the Town Hall clock ticking boredly. Pigeons crooning by the clock, perched on tender pink feet. Pigeons dropping to run among the stalls. Large-eyed pigeons. Running pigeons. In the mortuary the body of a man who was not cremated or buried. A man with arms. A man with hands. A man with fingers and skin on the fingers. A man whose finger-skin was being printed by another man, who kept breathing in starts. While other men waited in other places to see what the finger-skin would print. All in the early evening of Friday. Night in Russia. Day in America.

*   *   *

Brennan went up the stairs at H.Q., knocked on a door, went through the door. The room behind the door was Whitaker's office and the room seemed crowded, so that Brennan hesitated. Then he went forward to the desk and placed on it an attaché case he had been carrying. He opened the case, took out a file, took two cards from the file. He handed the two cards to Gently. Gently was sitting behind the desk. Beside Gently were sitting Campling and Whitaker and beside Campling sat Empton. Felling stood to the left of Whitaker. Madsen and Wanda Lane sat facing the desk. The two detective-constables, Rice and Freeman, stood towards the door, behind Wanda Lane.

Brennan said: 'These are the dabs, sir, and these are the ones we got at Huxford.'

Gently laid them side by side, looked from one to the other. 'You've made a comparison?' he asked.

'I made a quick one,' Brennan said. 'I counted seven points of similarity, sir, using a four-inch pocket magnifier. I also measured the height of the subject and looked for the scar on the left knee.'

'Did you find the scar?' Gently asked.

'Yes sir,' Brennan said. 'It's Sawney all right.'

The others looked at the two cards. Empton had hold of them last. He brought out his nest of magnifiers, used the desk lamp, used pins as pointers. At last he brushed the pins away and pocketed the magnifiers with a shrug. Gently looked across at Felling.

'Anything to tell us?' he asked.

Felling's heavy face was paled, he was clasping his hands behind his back.

'It's a bloody mystery to me, sir,' he said. 'That's all I can say about that. I took his prints, Freeman was with me. Freeman knows I took his prints.'

Gently picked up another card. 'Is this your signature here?' he asked.

Felling glanced over the card. 'Looks as though it might be mine,' he said.

'Yes, but is it?' Gently said. 'Take a good look at it and tell me.'

Felling took the card. His hand was unsteady. He didn't seem to see what he was looking at. He handed it back.

'Could be, sir. I'm not going to swear that it's mine. Like I said, it's a bloody mystery, but Freeman knows I took those prints.'

'What you're saying,' Gently said, 'is that someone switched this card for the genuine one? That someone had access to the blanks? That someone forged your signature accurately?'

'Well, what else could it be?' Felling said.

'Between the time,' Gently said, 'when you took the prints, and the time you compared them with Teodowicz' record?'

'It must have been done,' Felling said. 'That's the only explanation.'

Gently shook his head. 'I don't think so. There's another explanation, Felling.'

'Well, I don't know what it is,' Felling said. 'I took his prints, I bloody know that.'

'You also identified the body. With Madsen.'

Felling pulled his head back, didn't say anything.

'I can add to that,' Gently said, 'that somehow I didn't get to hear of this cremation. And somehow Madsen's prints were found in Teodowicz' flat to support Madsen's story about destroying the documents. That's two sets of prints with something queer about them, two curious facts that need explaining. I could add some other pointers if I thought it worth while.'

'What are you trying to get at,' Felling said. 'I could bring a case for defamation of character.'

'That's enough of that sort of talk, Felling,' Whitaker said. 'It stands out a mile, man. Your goose is cooked.'

'It's a lot of lies, 'Felling said. 'He can't prove a thing, sir.'

'It's self-evident!' Whitaker snapped. 'Shut your mouth, I'm bloody ashamed of you.'

'I'm going to have my lawyer,' Felling said.

Whitaker looked at Felling. Felling was silent.

'Any comment?' Gently said to Wanda.

Wanda's mouth was bitter. Her chin was lifted.

'Or from you?' Gently said to Madsen.

Madsen gave him a shrinking smile.

'All right then,' Gently said. 'I'll do the talking, since none of you seem to want to begin. And while I'm talking it may occur to you that there isn't much point in keeping silent. Because I'm going to charge each one of you three with being an accessory to Sawney's murder, and if you were accessories after the fact it'll be up to you to convince me of it. You know the ropes. What you say after this may be taken down and used in evidence. Freeman, put a chair there for Felling.'

'I don't want your chair,' Felling said.

'Put one there all the same,' Gently said. 'Stand over in front of it, Felling, whether you sit or not.'

'I'm not going over there,' Felling said. 'I'm not in this, it's a bloody frame-up.'

'Much more of it,' Whitaker said, 'and I'll have you hand-cuffed. Get over there, Felling. Get in that chair.'

Felling lounged across to the chair, pretended to dust it, sat, sprawled his legs. He looked at Wanda. Wanda didn't look at him. He looked at Madsen, Madsen dropped his eyes.

'Now,' Gently said. 'This is a crime arising out of the racket at Huxford. Why it took this particular form of violence is something not quite clear. That doesn't matter, from a prosecution viewpoint, we shall get a conviction just the same. But from another viewpoint it matters a great deal: from the viewpoint of political implication. Teodowicz is a Pole. He is a political refugee. He had received some overtures from the Polish authorities. It may be that as a result of threats from this quarter he took the course that he did take. If that's the case, we want to know it. We want to expel the people responsible. We want to make representations to the Polish authorities to try to prevent the same thing happening again. And conversely, if the Polish authorities had an innocent part in this, we want to establish that, too. We need to know. And I'm pretty certain that one of you is able to tell us.'

166

He broke off, looked from one to another of them. Nobody volunteered to speak. Felling was staring at the ceiling, his lips formed in a noisless whistle. Wanda's eyes bored at Gently. Madsen didn't raise his head. Madsen was leaning forward out of the chair, his fair complexion flushed.

'Very well,' Gently said. 'You probably still think I'm bluffing. So I'll just run through the course of events to let you see where you all stand. Sawney and Teodowicz were operating a racket in stores stolen from Huxford. Sawney obtained possession of the stores by fraud and Teodowicz collected and disposed of them. You probably knew of this, Mrs. Lane, but there is no evidence to implicate you. You, Madsen, certainly knew of it, and I think we shall be able to implicate you. And you, Felling, are self-evidently implicated. You knew of the racket. You were drawing a cut from it.'

'Oh I was, was I?' Felling said. 'You'd better see if you can prove it, hadn't you?'

'Certainly,' Gently said. 'Why else were you part of this conspiracy to aid Teodowicz? There can be only one reason. Teodowicz had it in his power to inform on you. Because of that you took the risks which have put you in the position you now occupy.' He picked up a paper from the desk. 'How much do you have in your current account, Felling?'

'To hell with my current account,' Felling said.

'You have over six hundred pounds,' Gently said. 'Would you care to explain where that came from?'

'Why should I explain it?' Felling said. 'I can win a bit at racing sometimes, can't I?'

'Oh, just keep quiet, man,' Whitaker said. 'I used to credit you with some intelligence.'

'It's a bloody lie,' Felling said. 'And nobody's going to make anything else of it.'

Wanda Lane said: 'It's the bloody truth. You make me sick. You blackmailed Tim.'

'Shut up, you tart,' Felling said.

Wanda turned her head to spit. She didn't say anything else. Felling sat scowling at his fists. Sweat was shining on his face.

'I'll continue,' Gently said. 'Sawney was in a false position. It was Teodowicz who handled the money, Sawney who would have to answer the questions. Teodowicz was trying to squeeze Sawney. Sawney resisted. They quarrelled over it. Then Sawney threatened to do something which, as it turned out, became his death warrant.' Gently looked at Madsen. 'What was that thing, Madsen?' he asked.

'I don' know,' Madsen said, shivering. 'I don' know anything about all this.'

'I think you do,' Gently said. 'I think you know more than anyone.'

'No,' Madsen said, 'no. I don' listen, I don' hear nothing.'

'I'll jog your memory,' Gently said. 'Sawney threatened to talk to a certain Stephan Razek.'

Madsen dug his chin in his chest, wouldn't look towards Gently.

'Sawney knew Razek,' Gently said, 'when Razek was at Huxford during the war. Razek is at present on attachment in this country and somehow Sawney must have got to know about it. He threatened to tell Razek of Teodowicz' whereabouts. On the surface this wasn't a very serious threat. It led only to Teodowicz being approached and urged to return to Poland to stand trial. This sort of thing has happened before and there seems nothing particularly sinister about it. People have resisted these approaches and there have been few attempts at coercion. But with Teodowicz it was different. He met the threat with a savage crime. He engineered a disappearance for himself intended to prevent all further pursuit. It follows that such a course was necessary to him, and we know that he had planned it in outline beforehand.

168

But we don't know why. And we need to know it.' Gently stared at Madsen. 'Why?' he asked.

'No,' Madsen said, 'no!' He squirmed in the chair, hunched over his knees.

'Are you afraid?' Gently said. 'Is that it?'

'I don' know about Tim's affairs!' Madsen said.

Wanda Lane said: 'Leave him alone. You don't think Tim would tell him anything, do you?'

'I don't think he'd tell anyone anything,' Gently said. 'But Madsen knows. He had the opportunity to know.'

'Tim told me,' Wanda said. She glared at the men behind the desk. 'But you bastards will never get it out of me. Not while Tim's alive,' she said.

'Listen to the whore,' Felling said.

'You keep quiet!' Whitaker snapped.

'Bloody why should I?' Felling said.

'I should, old fellow,' Empton said.

Felling was quiet. Nobody else said anything.

'We come to the mechanics of it,' Gently said. 'Teodowicz had a Sten gun and ammunition from Huxford. I don't think he obtained it with the intention of shooting Sawney, I think it was insurance against this factor we don't know about. Perhaps you'll tell us how long Teodowicz had it, Madsen?'

'Yes,' Madsen said. 'That is right, for some time. Tim say he would like to have a weapon of some sort, Sawney say all right, he can fix him with a gun.'

'How long ago?'

'Oh, one, two years,' Madsen said. 'Tim like the gun, he is often playing with it.'

'Did Tim say what the gun was for?'

Madsen shrank a little. 'He don' say that.'

'So,' Gently said, 'Teodowicz had the gun, and he could easily arrange for Sawney to meet him. He had only to say he had some money for him for Sawney to come running.

He rang him up, appointed a meeting in the car park behind Baddesley station. That was where he wanted Sawney's van found when it was discovered that Sawney was missing. Then he rang the guardroom at Huxford and gave them an annonymous tip-off about Sawney, providing at once the reason for Sawney's flight and grounds for suspecting Sawney of the crime to follow. He met Sawney, he killed or disabled him, exchanged clothes with him, drove him to the lay-by. There he inflicted such injuries on him with the gun that identification would be doubtful. He sent a final burst from bushes to suggest the van having been ambushed, then he escaped through the fields to The Raven, where his hiding place was prepared. About a mile distant, over the fields, a car was waiting for the final stage, but in the meantime he had to remain on the spot to ensure that his colleagues did their job. Mrs. Lane was completely under his influence, but Felling and Madsen only under duress. He needed to be there as a perpetual threat to prevent any treachery on their part. He had also some loose ends to tidy. Some documents remained in his handwriting. He destroyed these without informing Felling, which gave Felling a little trouble later on. You didn't burn those papers, did you, Madsen?'

'That is right,' Madsen said. 'I don' burn them.'

'You lying bastard,' Felling said. 'You bloody know you did burn them.'

'Why should he have burned them?' Gently said. 'Madsen didn't have any tracks to cover. But Teodowicz did. And his handwriting was part of them. That's how it was, wasn't it, Madsen?'

'The handwriting, I think so,' Madsen said.

'Because it wasn't the handwriting of Teodowicz,' Gently said. 'There isn't any Teodowicz. The real Teodowicz is dead. He disappeared way back in Poland, he never set foot outside that country.'

'No,' Madsen said. 'I can't say about that.'

'Yes, but you can,' Gently said. 'You heard the threat Sawney made to Teodowicz. Sawney knew Teodowicz' real identity.'

'No.' Madsen said. 'No. No.'

'Why don't you stop getting at him?' Wanda Lane said. 'Tim had to burn those papers because they linked him with Sawney.'

Gently shook his head. 'That's ruled out,' he said. 'Felling saw the papers. He would have burned them himself if they had connected Teodowicz with Sawney.'

'Felling is dumb.'

'Shut your trap,' Felling said.

'Or he didn't get a chance to burn them,' Wanda said. 'You're crazy about Tim being somebody else. You're guessing about it and you're guessing wrong.'

'Am I guessing wrong, Madsen?' Gently said.

'It's a hoot, the way you're kidding yourself,' Wanda said. 'So Tim did for that rat Sawney, and you know why. Isn't that enough for you?'

'Not when you're protesting so much,' Gently said.

'Oh, you're too bloody clever,' Wanda said. 'But you're not as clever as Tim, he's always two jumps ahead of you.'

'At the moment, about half a jump,' Gently said.

'And you had him surrounded,' Wanda said. 'Go on being clever. Call in the Navy and the Air Force. You won't catch Tim in a month of Sundays.'

She folded her thin arms, stared past them out of the window. Felling's face had a fixed sneer, but his eyes were empty. Madsen kept facing the floor. His lips worked with little smiles. He was wearing thick rough boots, the toes of which were turned together.

'So Sawney was dead,' Gently said. 'And Teodowicz and the gun were at The Raven. And Mrs. Lane knew the score, if she didn't know it earlier. But you, Madsen, knew it earlier, before that handy trip to Glasgow. You had to be intimidated into playing your part, and you had to know what it was when you returned. Isn't that so?'

Madsen smiled at his boots.

'So you're an accessory before the fact,' Gently said. 'And it goes without saying that Felling is too. Felling was to be first on the scene, he had to switch the fingerprint cards. He had to make certain that no doubts arose as to the identity of the body. Then he had to steer Madsen through the questioning and deflect interest away from The Raven. Felling was evidently briefed thoroughly, and briefed before the crime took place.'

'You'll say I did it in a minute,' Felling said. 'It's all lies, the bloody lot of it.'

'Felling,' Gently said, 'you'd better help us. It's the only sensible thing you can do.'

'Yes, I'll be a mug,' Felling said. 'I'll admit all them lies. Only I don't bloody think so. You don't catch me like that.'

'God, man, how can you be so stupid?' Whitaker said.

'Very funny,' Felling said. 'Only I'm innocent, that's what. I'm going to prove it, what's more, and then I'm going to sue that bastard. I'll teach him to come here with his slanders. I nearly let fly at him this afternoon.'

'Yes,' Gently said, 'you nearly did that, didn't you? And you were tempted in the garage yesterday, when I saw the significance of that oil bottle. But you're not a killer Felling. You're a treacherous fool, but you're not a killer. Try a little savvy now. Tell us what you know about Teodowicz.'

'You go to hell,' Felling said.

'You're going to catch a stiff one,' Gently said.

'If I catch it,' Felling said. 'You go to hell. There's no mug here.'

'All right, Felling,' Gently said. He looked at Wanda.

Wanda looked out of the window. 'You're not a killer either,' Gently said to her. 'You tried to protect me back there. But the man you're shielding is a killer: a psychopath and a killer. Don't fool yourself, Mrs. Lane. He'd have killed you too when it suited his purpose.'

'What do you know about Tim?' Wanda said.

'I know a lot about killers,' Gently said. 'They're lonely people, they daren't trust anyone. And so they're never to be trusted. Once a man goes through that gate he leaves all common claim behind him. His way back leads by the gallows or by what penalty the law provides. Until then he acts humanity like a wolf in a sheepskin. But he doesn't have it. He's an exile. When the wind blows on him, he'll kill again. If you know where Teodowicz is going, then tell us, Mrs. Lane.'

'You don't know Tim,' Wanda said. 'You think he's some petty criminal. Some Christie or Haig, those are the killers you know. Because you aren't big enough to understand him. Because you're pigmies and think like pigmies. Because you can't imagine a man who can kill and stay clean. But Tim is that sort of man. He can do what none of you would dare to. He has a right to take life because his soul doesn't shrink from it. And I'm telling you nothing about him, you can do your own clumsy chasing. Get your dogs and your cordons out and bring him in. If you can.'

'You're lucky,' Gently said, 'that you're here.'

'Thank you for nothing,' Wanda said.

Gently shrugged, looked at Madsen. 'What about you, Madsen?' he said. 'You aren't serving the Christ child with a Sten gun in his hand.'

Madsen was trembling. He looked towards Gently. His pale eyes flickered, came to a stare.

'Yes,' he said. 'Ver' well, ver' well.'

'Filthy traitor!' Wanda shouted.

Madsen looked at her, twisting his lips. 'Not a traitor,' he said. 'That man is too wicked.'

She spat on his cheek. He kept trying to smile. 'No, not a traitor,' he repeated.

*   *   *

Madsen spoke in a low voice so that he had to be listened to with care. The colour in his cheeks came and went, he didn't know what to do with his eyes. Wanda had turned her back on him. She sat motionless, hands in lap. Freeman had moved up close to her. She paid no attention when he moved up. Felling glared all the while at Madsen, sat saggingly, had his fists on his thighs.

'Yes, it is right,' Madsen whispered. 'Tim didn' pay Sawney the proper money. This is why they have the row, it is all about the money. Sawney is ver' angry with Tim, I think they maybe have a fight. But no, not a fight, they begin to say what they are to do to each other. Tim say he will tell the Air Force people if Sawney does not like what he gets. Sawney say, either he get the money or he will fix Tim for good and all. Tim say, what does he mean by that. Sawney laugh at him, sound ver' nasty, say he will tell a little bird where Tim is living just now. I don't care about that, Tim say. But yes, you will care, Sawney say. Then he get out his wallet and show Tim a picture that come out of a newspaper.'

'Did you see that picture?' Gently asked.

Madsen nodded. 'Yes. I see it. Is a ver' old picture, I think, come out of a newspaper during the war. There is Tim in the middle in a ver' smart suit, and two Totenkopf officers, you know, the S.S. They are smiling, ver' pleased. It say something underneath in Polish. But it is Tim all right, I can see that at a glance.'

'How did Teodowicz take it?' Gently asked.

'Is frightened, I think,' Madsen said. 'He look at the picture become ver' quiet. Then he ask Sawney where he get the picture. Sawney say, from someone who knew Tim, someone who is killed during the war. He was a Jew, Sawney say, he was going to kill Tim after the war. And there is another one, Sawney tell him, and he does not die during the war, he is here, in this country, he would like ver' much to know about Tim. And all the Poles, Sawney say, they would like to know about Tim too. Or about someone else, he say, pointing to the picture. Then he call Tim by another name.'

'What other name?' Gently said.

Madsen touched his forehead. 'I try to think,' he said. 'It is a simple name, ver' simple. Perhaps it come to me, I don' know. But Tim look terrible when Sawney say it. That is not so, he say. I am Teodowicz, I have my papers, the British police have checked about me. Sawney say, then that is all right, the Poles don' care about Teodowicz. So do I get my money, Sawney say. Tim say he'll think about that, don' have the money by him. Don' think too long, Sawney say, no Polish bastard is going to gyp me. And then he go out, and that is all. Is the last time I see Sawney.'

'But the name?' Gently said.

'Is ver' simple,' Madsen said. 'But I am frightened. Tim frighten me. He say he kill me if I remember. When Sawney is gone he get out the gun, keep playing with it, looking at me. I am ver' scared, you understand? I know he kill me in a minute. It is right, you cannot trust them, they are not men any more. I think he has done some terrible things. I don' want to know what he has done.'

'He'll be caught,' Gently said. 'You needn't be frightened of him any more.'

'Is silly name,' Madsen said. 'Like big, or thick, name like that.'

Empton looked up at the ceiling. 'Could it be like Slin?' he asked. 'Nickolaus Slin?'

'But yes, that is it,' Madsen said. 'That is the name Sawney says—Nickolaus Slin.'

They all looked at Empton. He was smoking one of his cigarettes. He didn't bother to look at them, slanted smoke towards the ceiling.

'Well, well,' he said. 'Fancy that. And everyone thought he was in South America. This is a blow for Rule Britannia —or will be, when it gets around.'

'You know who it is?' Whitaker said.

'But of course, old man,' Empton said. 'Slin was mayor of Grodz during the occupation, one of Heinie's blue-eyed boys. Not quite a celebrity, by current standards. His score is reckoned at twenty thousand.'

'Twenty thousand what?' Whitaker said.

'Jews,' Empton said. 'What else? He set up some ovens at Dolina, outside Grodz, with a top capacity of about five hundred a week. A very moderate performer, I suppose, but his memory is still kept green in Poland. He'd disappeared when the Russians got there. A lot of talent has been questing for Slin.'

'My God,' Whitaker said. He repeated it.

'Now we know the whole story,' Empton said. 'Slin did away with a black marketeer called Teodowicz and took his identity, and migrated here. It looks as though little Jan were telling the truth. They would hardly have sent a man to talk to Slin. Sawney must have tipped them without telling them who it was; but of course, the mildest attention would be too much for Slin.' He puffed some smoke, glanced down at Madsen. 'You wouldn't have lived, old fellow,' he said. 'Nor would Felling, if he knew about it. Nor would the magnificent Mrs. Lane.'

Wanda turned to look at Empton. 'You're muck,' she said. 'Just muck.'

'Nicely taken,' Empton said. 'What a gift you have for timing.'

'You'll never get Tim,' Wanda said. 'The Russians couldn't. Nobody can. He's out of the reach of amateurs like you. He'll go where he wants to. Nobody can stop him.'

'So he's going somewhere, is he?' Empton said.

Wanda snapped her thin lips.

'Good,' Empton said. 'We'll watch the ports and airfields. Especially the stuff going west. Yet,' he said, 'that will scarcely be necessary. I think we can do better than that. I'll have a little chat with our friend Razek—you know how it is? Set a Pole to catch a Pole.'

'Muck,' Wanda said. 'Just muck.'

Empton chuckled. 'I like you,' he said. He looked at his watch. 'Think I'll get along,' he said. 'I'm sure the legal routine is in good hands.'

He nodded to Gently. Whitaker rose. Campling continued to sit saying nothing.

POLISH GUNMAN'S CAR FOUND

WATCH ON DOCK AREA

The car known to have been driven by Timoshenko Teodowicz, the armed Pole wanted by the police in connection with the A1 shooting incident, was discovered yesterday in a cul-de-sac in the Highfield district of Southampton. Police wearing revolvers were today patrolling the dock area of the town and tracker dogs have been used.

* * *

SOUTHAMPTON MAN'S CAR AT MARBLE ARCH

MR. EDWARD STOCKBRIDGE

When Mr. Edward Stockbridge of 21, Calcutta Road, went to collect his car after a visit to the Gaumont Cinema last night, he could not find the car. This morning the Town Police contacted Mr. Stockbridge to tell him that his car had been found—near the Marble Arch. The Metropolitan Police, not knowing it to be stolen, had towed it away to their 'pound'. Mr. Stockbridge has been assured that he will not be fined on this occasion.

GUNMAN'S WEAPON FOUND
STEN GUN IN STREAM
CHILDREN PADDLING FIND IT

Two small boys yesterday found the weapon used in the A1 shooting incident, for which the police have been searching since Tuesday. The boys are Eric Blanton, aged 7, and Thomas Seggs, aged 8, of Compton, Hampshire. They found the gun while they were paddling in the River Itchen, near their home. Police think that Teodowicz jettisoned the gun while he was making his way to Southampton.

* * *

COSH BANDIT SOUGHT
ATTACKS IN DALSTON AREA

Police are searching for a heavily-built man of about 50 who they think is responsible for several recent cosh attacks in the Dalston area. The man, who may be a foreigner, chooses victims as they are leaving public houses. He has got away with amounts of from £2 to £37.

* * *

FELLING: 6 YEARS
MADSEN: 'IN GRAVE FEAR'
CONDITIONAL DISCHARGE FOR WANDA LANE

Sentencing ex-Detective Sergeant Ronald Felling (40) to six years' imprisonment for his part in the A1 shooting incident, at Offingham Assizes today, the Judge, Mr. Justice Ashley, described him as 'a thoroughly corrupt individual who had made no bones about betraying the trust society had placed in him.' Of Ove Madsen (39), who received a sentence of one year's imprisonment, the Judge said: 'He is not a strong character and he went in grave fear of that terrible man. I believe this is an instance when the clemency of English Justice should be shown.' Giving the third defendent, Wanda Lane (36), a conditional discharge, Mr. Justice Ashley said of her that: 'She was patently under the influence of Teodowicz, and I can see no purpose in adding to her misery by sentencing her to a term in prison. I intend to give her another chance to see if she can work out her salvation.'

*　　　*　　　*

OWLES, STANGATE & OLIVER

For Sale, By Order of The Proprietor

The Raven roadhouse, situated in a commanding position on the A1, 2m. south of Everham, and consisting of an excellent Chalet-style timber building comprising 12 Bedrooms, 2 baths & etc., residents Lounge & Dining Rooms, Cafeteria & well-fitted Kitchen, private Parlour & Bedrooms; extensive Car Park with Petrol Pump installation (3 pumps), large Kitchen Garden with Poultry Run & matured Fruit-trees, Fuel-store, Outbuildings & etc. By Auction at The Lamb Hotel, Offingham, Oct. 27.

*　　　*　　　*

PROPERTY MARKET

Messrs. Owles, Stangate & Oliver offered a varied selection of properties for sale at The Lamb Hotel, Offingham, yesterday. They included The Raven roadhouse, Everham, £1300 (Mr. George, for a client). . . .

PUBLICAN ATTACKED

XMAS CLUB FUNDS STOLEN

An intruder with a cosh last night attacked Mr. Percy Billington (51), licensee of The Black Boy Public House, Norton Street, Stoke Newington, and got away with nearly £200 of Xmas Club funds. The attack occurred soon after closing time when Mr. Billington was making up the club ledger. Police believe that the intruder had concealed himself in the toilets.

*   *   *

Wednesday December 24th. Big Ben striking four times. A gloomy mist settled in Whitehall and over the muddy tides of the Thames. The great exodous proceeding by way of traffic jams and crawling trains. Frost forecast. Frost apparent in the sparkle of the lights in County Hall.

Gently looked around his office, pulled on his coat, wrapped his scarf. The basket was emptied, the desk neat, the trays vacant, the chairs aligned. The calendar read two days in advance, Saturday December 26th: he had pulled a string in the A.C's office and two days had grudgingly been given him. Bridget, his sister, was spending Christmas with him, and along with Bridget her son and daughter-in-law. He would be meeting them in the Leicester Square Corner House in twenty minutes and later they were going to the Coliseum. A Christmas break. He looked round again. The office was warm, tidy and bare. He stuck his pipe in his mouth, reached for the door handle. The telephone rang. He looked at it, sucking.

He went to the desk, picked up the phone.

'Yes?'

'Hullo, old man.' It was Empton. 'Hoped I should catch

you,' Empton said. 'I've just come in from something amusing.'

'I'm just leaving,' Gently said.

'Shan't keep you a moment,' Empton said. 'It's to do with our Polish expedition, remember? The bloke who fired his gun so much.'

'What about him?' Gently said.

'He's in the morgue,' Empton said. 'We found him stiff and stark in Hackney. He'd been holing up there since last August.'

Gently sucked. 'How did it happen?'

'Gas,' Empton said. 'In his bedroom.'

'Was it suicide?'

'Not quite,' Empton said. 'The door had been sealed on the outside. There was a rubber tube led in from the kitchen and poked underneath the door. He'd got the window closed, of course, the nights being rather chill. A very crisp little job. No prints, no witnesses.'

'Do you know who did it?' Gently asked.

'But of course, old man,' Empton said. 'Nothing we can prove in the C.C.C., but we don't do much of that in our line of business. Watch your papers after Christmas.'

'Was it this Razek?' Gently said.

'Strictly *sub judice*,' Empton said. 'But you can draw any conclusions that seem good to you.' He paused, and Gently heard him chuckle. 'You remember Mrs. Lane?' he said.

'Yes.'

'She was with him,' Empton said. 'Two single beds. She was on the other one.'

'She was dead too?' Gently said.

'Yes, strangled,' Empton said. 'Yesterday, according to the medic. Been dead for thirty-six hours.'

Gently stared out at the mist. 'Any clothes on the body?'

'None,' Empton said. 'Damned un-bourgeois, wasn't it? Merry Christmas, old man.'

DIPLOMAT DECLARED PERSONA NON GRATA

'UNDESIRABLE ACTIVITIES'

TO LEAVE WITHIN 24 HOURS

*   *   *

And that was all, and soon forgotten in the scattered annals of the Road. The man who died there was briefly noticed because some people wanted to murder his killer. Not that it mattered very much, even in the country where it happened. People were being killed there every day without it being of great consequence. Certainly it mattered not at all to, say, the larger countries round about, and had no register beyond the Sun and in the less-trivial galaxies. Man is interesting but a little remote, and perhaps over-suicidal to be taken seriously. A terminal brightness in a dull corner may be his fraction of sidereal consequence. For he is seeded with self-destruction, he has a fuse of pride to his nations. He is a small race on a small planet and has the assertion-to-death of small creatures. He is a foolish animal without the law and his extinction merely curious. He was probably a biological mistake which fortunately was self-correcting. His vision extended North and South. But he saw nothing beside the Road.

Brundall, 1961